Dorothy L. Sayers

The Centenary Celebration

Dorothy L. Sayers

The Centenary Celebration

EDITED BY

ALZINA STONE DALE

WALKER AND COMPANY

NEW YORK

First published in the United States of America in 1993 by Walker
Publishing Company, Inc.

Published simultaneously in Canada by Thomas Allen & Son Canada,
Limited, Markham, Ontario

Library of Congress Cataloging-in-Publication Data
Dorothy L. Sayers : the centenary celebration / edited and introduced
by Alzina Stone Dale.
p.   cm.
ISBN 0-8027-3224-0
1. Sayers, Dorothy L. (Dorothy Leigh), 1893–1957—Criticism and
interpretation. 2. Detective and mystery stories, English—History
and criticism. 3. Wimsey, Peter (Fictitious character) I. Sayers,
Dorothy L. (Dorothy Leigh), 1893–1957. II. Dale. Alzina Stone.
1931–   .
PR6037.A95Z646   1993
823'.912—dc20   92-44894
CIP

Book design by Shelli Rosen

Printed in the United States of America

2   4   6   8   10   9   7   5   3   1

"Dorothy L. Sayers: Biography Between the Lines," by Carolyn G. Heilbrun. Reprinted
from *The American Scholar* 51, no. 4 (Autumn 1982). Copyright © 1982 by the author.
"A Personal Memoir: Dorothy L. Sayers," by Michael Gilbert. Copyright © 1993 by Michael
Gilbert.
"D. L. S.: An Unsteady Throne?" by Ian Stuart. Copyright © 1993 by Ian Stuart.
"Butler, Dabbler, Spy: Jeeves to Wimsey to Bond," by William F. Love. Copyright © 1993
by William F. Love.
"*Gaudy Night*: Quintessential Sayers," by Carolyn G. Hart. Copyright © 1993 by Carolyn G.
Hart.
"The Marriage of True Minds," by B. J. Rahn. Copyright © 1993 by B. J. Rahn.
"*Thrones, Dominations*: Unfinished Testament to Friendship?" by Alzina Stone Dale. Copy-
right © 1993 by Alzina Stone Dale.
"It Was the Cat!" by Catherine Aird. Copyright © 1993 by Catherine Aird.
"Where the Bodies Are Buried: The Real Murder Cases in the Crime Novels of Dorothy L.
Sayers," by Sharyn McCrumb. Copyright © 1993 by Sharyn McCrumb.
"The Art of Framing Lies: Dorothy L. Sayers on Mystery Fiction," by Aaron Elkins. Copy-
right © 1993 by Aaron Elkins.
"Dorothy L. Sayers on Dante," by Anne Perry. Copyright © 1993 by Anne Perry.
"Unsoothing Sayers," by Ralph McInerny. Copyright © 1993 by Ralph McInerny.
"Dorothy L.'s Mickey Finn," by H. R. F. Keating. Copyright © 1993 by H. R. F. Keating.
"The Comedy of Dorothy L. Sayers," by Catherine Kenney. Copyright © 1993 by Catherine
Kenney.

FOR RACHEL MARSHALL GOETZ

Lifelong friend and mentor who not only shares her birthday—June 13—with Dorothy L. Sayers but also was responsible for my career as a writer.

Contents

Contents

Acknowledgments

I WOULD LIKE TO THANK my friend Harry Keating, the editor of *Agatha Christie, First Lady of Crime,* for doing a festschrift for a "mere" mystery writer, because his book gave me the idea for mine. I also want to thank all the other contributors here and abroad for entering into the project with a Sayersian enthusiasm and for being so blessedly prompt with their pieces. In return, I have tried not to edit them but let them speak their minds in their own ways.

Several other mystery mavens encouraged me to do the project, particularly Janet Rudolph of Mystery Readers International and Kathy Daniels of *The Armchair Detective.* I also owe a great deal to the organizers of Malice Domestic, where I was able to meet other mystery writers and orchestrate the project.

Once again, old friends rallied to help me, especially Marilyn Roth of the Bridgman Public Library and Acting Curator Marjorie Lamp Mead of the Wade Center at Wheaton College. Finally, my agent, Robin Rue, believed in the worth of the work and made it happen. Taken altogether, this book is a fitting tribute to Sayers and her own circle of friends, all of whom were relentlessly drawn into whatever activity she was working on.

—*Alzina Stone Dale*

Introduction:
A Jury of Her Peers

THIS BOOK IS A TRIBUTE to a very special person, Dorothy L. Sayers. Born four years before Queen Victoria's Diamond Jubilee, when, in her words, "it seemed as if the sun would never set upon the vast British Empire," Sayers would have been one hundred years old on June 13, 1993. Although she died in 1957, there has been no loss of interest in her or her works; on the contrary, there has been a steady outpouring of books about Sayers, which have added to our understanding of her, even when the books offer widely differing viewpoints.

Sayers's own work has never been out of print, and new readers discover her every day. Many of her fans reread her books, the sure sign, according to her friend C. S. Lewis, of a classic. Clearly, something about her still appeals. From these essays, it appears that there is a je ne sais quoi in Sayers's unmistakable voice, which reveals her, still "alive in her work," as well as her talent as a "maker and craftsman."

As a professional writer, Sayers was justly proud of being a jack-of-all-trades; she wrote mysteries, poetry, essays, reviews, and plays, and first "translated" the New Testament, then Dante's *Divine Comedy*, into modern colloquial English. Sayers was also enthusiastically and energetically interested in her craft. She not only shared her work in progress with her fellow artists and close friends, but she was a founder and sturdy supporter of the Detection Club, which still exists chiefly to let its members eat dinner together and talk shop.

It seemed obvious that the only way to celebrate her work was to ask a jury of her peers to judge it. As a happy result, I gathered here a baker's dozen of writers, each in his or her own way telling what Sayers's writing has meant for theirs. I felt that no other kind of tribute would have appealed to her so much, but I did not try to load the decks in her favor. After all, Sayers herself was famous for her defense of the mystery's rules of fair play. It is fitting that several writers disagree heartily about her good points, and one is a downright naysayer, echoing the opinion of many who call her a pedantic snob. It is a representative jury: there are nearly as many men as women, a rough equality between the United Kingdom and the United States, and several mystery writers who preferred to focus on nonmysterious aspects of Sayers's craft. Three of us are not mystery writers but have published critical or biographical books on Sayers.

These jurors talk about the ways that Sayers taught them their trade, and they value her as a truly awesome feminine role model. Not surprisingly, they tend to agree that Sayers knew her life and work were all of a piece, in which, looking "back along the sequence of her creatures . . . [she saw that] each was in some way the outcome and fulfillment of the rest—that all her worlds belong to the one universe."

In addition to describing her own world with particularity, these jurors also accuse Sayers of seeing the mystery as a morality play. They insist that she wrote about ethics and values, describing life in terms of good and evil—all concepts that had gone out of literary fashion but are getting a new lease on life in today's mystery fiction. Finally, to her honor, these writers include the present Ruler (or President) of the Detection Club, over which she once presided with a six-shooter hidden in her academic gown, past chairmen of the British Crime Writers Association, a Mystery Writers of America grand master, a former president of the Modern Language Association, a past president of Sisters in Crime, plus Edgar and Dagger winners galore. These are not humble beginners but lords and ladies of her realm.

For a professional writer who lived by her pen, this jury seemed just right. Let us devoutly hope she would think so. Sayers was not so much a "strange lady," as one early biographer called her, as a remarkable one; she was also a very formidable *dame* who never suffered fools gladly. Now I can understand that it was as much her fault as mine that I failed to meet her when we were both in London after World War II, but then, without even knowing it, she thoroughly squashed me from afar.

A young expatriate American, I was living in a chilly Bloomsbury bed and breakfast, writing a historical novel while I tried to decide whether to take the only jobs available to aliens—teaching in London's East End or washing dishes in the West End—or go home. I eagerly collected all Sayers's books secondhand in the Charing Cross bookstores, walked the bombed-out streets of her city, and debated with a college friend, Marie de Kiewiet, whether to write Sayers a fan letter. The two of us met daily for tea in the basement of the British Museum, where it was warm, often sharing it with other "colonials" but occasionally with a true Brit, who regarded us all as barbarians beyond the pale.

Before I even got up my nerve, Sayers wrote a very tart letter to the *Sunday Times* in which she snapped at students who wasted her time. My brash American gall totally failed me. Instead of writing her, I made a solitary pilgrimage to Mecklenberg Square the day before I sailed for home. There I stared wistfully at the tennis court, miraculously unbombed, where Harriet Vane had heard a game in progress in *Gaudy Night*. This book therefore represents a fitting finale to my personal "Sayers industry," from which I got my start in writing and gained entrée into the mystery field. Sayers's publisher once hyped Sayers as the "Queen of Crime," an appropriate enough title for one who greatly admired England's Elizabeth I as born to the right job and choosing to do it. Titles may be in jeopardy in England today, but there are plenty of present-day writers whose publishers are proud to claim their right to her succession. Long live the queen!

—*Alzina Stone Dale*

Dorothy L. Sayers

Biography Between the Lines

CAROLYN G. HEILBRUN
(AKA AMANDA CROSS)

For over a decade now, dedicated readers of the works of Dorothy L. Sayers have sought the story of her life in whatever clues presented themselves or could be scrounged up. In 1937 Sayers wrote to her son:

> People are always imagining that if they get hold of the writer himself and, so to speak, shake him long enough and hard enough, something exciting and illuminating will drop out of him. But it doesn't. What's due to come out has come out, in the only form in which it ever can come out. All one gets by shaking is the odd paper clip and crumpled carbons of his wastepaper basket. . . . What we make is more important than what we are, particularly if making is our profession.

But for women something exciting and illuminating may indeed drop out; the world is scarcely replete with models of female achievement. Long before it was known that Sayers had had an illegitimate child, or fallen passionately in love with a scoundrel, or married a neurasthenic veteran of World War I, readers had guessed at the great intelligence, the devotion to craft, and, above all, the sense of vocation that rings, bell-like, throughout her writing. There is some question (to which I shall return) as to whether in the end, as C. S. Lewis guessed, Sayers's devotion to her "proper job" became an excuse for suiting herself; but in the earlier years, the years of the detective novels, her concept of doing one's own work and not someone else's was a powerful idea for women, who had always been persuaded to make someone else their job.

Readers, responding to this sense of vocation, naturally wished to examine the text of Sayers's life. When her heirs—her son, Anthony Fleming, and her agent, David Higham—at first refused an authorized biography, the result was several American biographies, sound but incomplete, and one English one, unsound, unfair, and distressing. Awakened to the problem, her executors commissioned a biography. We now have, in James Brabazon's biography, published in 1981, the story of Dorothy Sayers's life, insofar as a readable and honest presentation of the available facts can offer it to us. James Brabazon has given us, with great clarity and fairness, all the events and dates and as many quotations from the voluminous sources as space allowed. It is a great compliment to his work that its comprehensiveness and honesty enables us to create, from his biography, a life story different from the one he thought to tell.

For, as one of Virginia Woolf's characters observed, it takes fifty pairs of eyes to see round that woman. Today, especially, biographies of women speak to women of their own lives; reading a biography, or writing one, we women write our own biographies between the lines. No longer confined to the erotic plot—the script already written by men for women by which women wait for maturity, marriage, motherhood, and, above all, for the chance to find their place in the destiny of a man—some women now look for other patterns, for possibilities of adventure, accomplishment, ambition. We seek to know about women whose lives include risk and the desire for individual achievement, as well as love. We have learned, in short, to search the accounts of women for exemplary lives: we need examples of female endeavor.

There is, of course, danger in this attempt. Since no one's life can be really known, since what is recorded or remembered very much depends on chance, as biographers and readers of biography, we all choose among the relics to form the life we want to envision for our subject. Roland Barthes has written that he finds biography offensive because it entails "a counterfeit integration of the subject."

Who can deny it? In choosing among biographies, we choose among counterfeit integrations. Perhaps in choosing the lives we lead, we do the same.

Let any woman imagine for a moment a biography of herself based upon those records she has left, those memories fresh in the minds of surviving friends, those letters that chanced to be kept, those impressions made, perhaps, on the biographer who was casually met in the subject's later years. What secrets, what virtues, what passions, what discipline, what fallings-out would, on the subject's death, become lost forever? How much has vanished or been distorted, even in our memories? Most of us tell ourselves stories of our past, make fictions of it, and these narrations *become* the past, the only part of our lives that is not submerged.

James Brabazon, like all biographers, has had to form his biography from what remains. But he has also formed it from his own interpretation of what a woman's life can be. Before discussing his biography of Dorothy Sayers, I ought, properly, to record my own relations to Sayers, my special narration (or version) of her life. It is impossible to overestimate the importance to me of her detective novels, through what should have been, but was not, a time of hope: this phrase, significantly, is used by C. P. Snow to characterize a young man's youth, when all seems possible, and his destiny awaits him if he will but set his feet upon the path. For the young woman, however, for whom the female destiny of flirtation, wedding, and motherhood is insufficient or even unattractive, youth is less a time of hope than a time of uncertainty, at worst a time of depression and a certain wild experimentation among the passions: as though, in watching male passions turned upon oneself, one could distract one's attention from the blunted female destiny. In such a time as this, I read Sayers, and through her wit, or intelligence, or portrayal of a female community and a moral universe, I caught sight of a possible life. Sayers provided a fantasy, of course—all detective novels are fantasies—but at least hers was not the romantic fantasy long prescribed for women.

In 1968, when I had indeed moved into a time of hope, I thought I understood Sayers's unique attractions and tried to capture them in a short essay. I got quite a few facts wrong (Sayers would have frowned with distaste), but I caught, I think, something of the spirit in her work that was evident to those who were drawn to her. Interestingly, some years later I was handed copies of her highly personal letters to a man who had scorned her. (James Brabazon has told the story in the *New York Times*, with the facts only slightly garbled after all these years.) What happened was far too unlikely for Sayers ever to have included it in one of her novels.

A man I did not know came to my office at Columbia University and asked me if I knew that the Houghton Library at Harvard possessed love letters from Dorothy Sayers to John Cournos. I did not know nor, I think, did anyone else outside the Houghton Library. This man had apparently chosen me to receive them because of my 1968 essay. Who he was or how he had acquired typed copies of the letters I did not ask and do not know. He simply handed them to me. The original letters had quite properly been closed to the public; I mentioned these letters to James Brabazon when he was working on his biography but did not show them to him. Copies of the handwritten originals were eventually turned over to him by the Houghton Library with the permission of Sayers's son.

The letters revealed a woman passionately in love, telling the man who had scorned her of a subsequent love affair, the conception and birth of her child, and her acquisition of a motorcycle. They presented a whole new view of Sayers: the troubled woman as opposed to the witty contriver I had previously invented. As I read these letters (I could not be certain they were not forgeries, but I did not believe they were, because the same voice from the novels spoke unmistakenly through them), I conceived a passionate desire to write Sayers's biography. I thought I had begun to understand her as a woman and as a writer. James Brabazon, however, was chosen for the task, and I believe the choice was the right one. He had two qualifications essential, as his work makes clear, for a biographer of Sayers: he is English, with that inherent understanding of a culture that cannot be learned, and he is conversant with and sympathetic to her religious beliefs. Apart from Brabazon's excuses for Sayers's anti-Semitism (to which I shall return) and a few minor quibbles, all my comments on Brabazon's biography are offered as addenda, not criticism. A biography by the first writer to have access to all of a person's papers must meet one absolute criterion: it must present factual material so as to assure the possibility of subsequent, and differing, interpretations. James Brabazon has fulfilled this qualification.

He has used two invaluable sources for his biography, apart from Sayers's letters: the thirty-three pages of an unpublished autobiography, *My Edwardian Childhood,* and the two hundred pages of an uncompleted novel, *Cat O'Mary,* clearly autobiographical and coinciding neatly with the facts revealed in *My Edwardian Childhood.* Brabazon has used these materials in his reconstruction of Sayers's early years. It is of particular interest to a woman contriver of female plots to notice that, although Sayers instructed her son to destroy all her papers, she herself had saved her letters to her parents (these are astonishingly open) and many childish compositions and drawings. Behind this lies, I would guess, not so much an unconscious wish for a posthumous biography (which she apparently did not want, even at an unconscious level) as a hope that she herself might, in her late, more leisurely years, reconstruct her life into a meaningful pattern and perceive within her struggles the outline of a destiny. As it happened, she died very suddenly at the age of sixty-four; happily for us, her son has preserved these materials.

Brabazon begins his biography not with Sayers's birth but with her sense of despair at the age of twenty-eight, when she was, in Brabazon's words, "a virgin and unemployed." We may notice that Brabazon puts the virginity first, but Sayers herself, writing to her parents, complains: "I can't get the work I want." In the list of deprivations that follows she mentions money, clothes, and a holiday—all before the man. Which is to say that I, as a woman, see the story differently from Brabazon but am enabled, by his integrity, to interpret it as I choose. He believes more than do I in the power of the erotic plot, male designed, in the life of an extraordinary woman.

Yet one must hasten to say that Brabazon is far from prejudiced in his presentation. What he has to deal with are Sayers's expressed opinions, and these uphold his interpretations of the events in her life. "For the most part," he writes, "she made the best—and the very good best—of the cards life dealt her." He suspects that Sayers might have been happier had she been pretty, "normally" married, with lots of children, had she not been a lonely, only child; "life robbed her of most of the ordinary human experiences of satisfactory emotional relationships, sexual and parental. No wonder she had to fall back on the intellect." He assumes that Sayers had "a raw deal" in not being "physically attractive and sure of herself in adolescence." In short, he asks for Sayers the accoutrement necessary for the successful enactment of a male-designed script. He recognizes, but does not endorse, the possibility that it is precisely not being sexually attractive in youth that enables women to develop the ego-strength to be creative and ultimately part of the instrumental rather than the expressive world in adulthood.

It is not Brabazon's maleness that leads to his interpretation of Sayers's real and possible happiness. As I have suggested elsewhere, men have long found it less difficult than have women to re-create imaginatively the constraints and pressures of a female life. More women than men biographers endorse the erotic plot for women as fulfilling; more women than men blame women subjects for avoiding a conventional life. And Brabazon is, in addition, right in recognizing that, at least in the last decades of her life, Sayers was deeply conventional.

Yet the early years are what count. Erik Erikson, while he concerns himself only with male lives, has helpfully identified the period known as the moratorium, which occurs in the lives of certain gifted persons—Shaw and William James are excellent examples. It is a time when the individual appears, before he is about thirty, to be getting nowhere, accomplishing none of his aims or altogether unclear as to what those aims might be. Such a person is, of course, actually preparing himself for the task that awaits him. For my purposes, Yeats is a clearer example of the opposition that appears between what the individual seems to want and what he or she in fact does to facilitate the as yet unrealized vocation. Yeats, at an even later age than Sayers, might have written that he was without work, money, sexual experience. In a way that seems perverse to many students of his work, Yeats fell in love with an unattainable woman even while desiring sexual love. Before Erikson, we were inclined to search for psychological restraints upon sexual expression. It is perhaps likelier that Yeats was providing himself with that experience essential to the poet he sought to become and that he lived the life suited to his vocation rather than to what he consciously recorded as his desires. I would suggest that there is a similar moratorium in Sayers's life. Loving an unobtainable man, rocketing from one unsatisfactory job to another, she was creating for herself a life sharply distinguished from the "normal" life of a young woman of her time. The constant sense of marking time and of lacking a goal, the love of a cad, the affair with the man who fathered her child, the secret birth and maintenance of that child—this was the fiction she was creating for her life, even as she appeared to be wasting time and suffering from profound frustration.

None of this is to suggest anything wrong or mistaken in Brabazon's interpretation; it is only to suggest that, with highly gifted women, as with men, their failure to lead the conventional life, to find the conventional way early, may signify more than the fact that they have been dealt a poor hand of cards. It may well be the forming of a life in the service of a gift or talent, felt but unrecognized and unnamed. This condition is marked by a profound sense of vocation, with no idea as to what that vocation is.

We can guess now that it was essential to Dorothy Sayers's sense of vocation that she put beyond reach the temptation of the conventional woman's life. By becoming pregnant at a time when that was (as it was to remain in Sayers's mind always) a great sin, by pouring out her love to a man incapable of receiving it, Sayers assured herself her strange independence. The letters to Cournos are particularly revealing of both her despair and the hints she seemed to catch of the possibilities that lay ahead. Brabazon is correct in discerning in Sayers a great desire for sexual experience: she wished not only to be desired but to achieve orgasm. In the largely unsatisfactory man who eventually became her husband, Sayers found both sexual satisfaction and independence. That Sayers's husband, Oswald Atherton Fleming ("Mac"), was damaged in the war made for his unhappiness but not hers, in a profound sense. We may even surmise that his refusal to allow her child to live with them suited, at some unconscious level, her own needs. Fulfilling the role society has assigned to the male more than Mac did, Sayers paid for her son's care, supervised his education, and went about her "proper job." Brabazon cleverly guesses that Mac, whatever his failings, was, at least in the early years of their marriage, good in bed.

Sayers's attitude toward her appearance in her later years confirms the sense that, once her moratorium was passed, she was free to disdain those efforts of dress, cosmetics, and hairdressing that had always caused her undue effort and dissatisfaction. The sense of conforming to the ideals of attractive womanhood is one that sustains many women in our culture as they grow older. To "let oneself go" is to resign one's sense of oneself as a woman, and therefore as a person. Women are, of course, rightly involved with their physical attractiveness, but for that reason it requires great courage to ignore one's appearance and reach out, as it were, from behind it to attract and spellbind; it also requires great talent. Ralph Hone has quoted in his biography (Brabazon does not) Mary Ellen Chase's account of Sayers's appearance in 1934, when she was only forty-one:

> There can be few plainer women on earth than Dorothy Sayers, and the adjective is an extremely kind one. She seemingly had no neck at all. Her head appeared to be closely joined to the regions directly between her shoulder blades in back and her collar bone in front. She had a florid complexion, very blue, near-sighted eyes, and wore glasses which quivered. Her thinning hair rarely showed evidence of care or forethought in its total lack of arrangement. . . . She was large, rawboned, and awkward.

Yet Chase—the woman frightened of unconventionality yet recognizing, perhaps even envying, the ultimate appeal—adds: "Just as I have never seen a less attractive woman to look upon, I have never come across one so magnetic to listen to." There were times when

Sayers, even in the late years, got herself up to look quite handsome. But can it be doubted that for a woman to grow fat in middle age is to disassociate her personhood from her feminine appeal? As Sayers was to write about women wearing trousers, answering men who criticized this unbecoming practice: "If the trousers do not attract you, so much the worse; for the moment I do not want to attract you. I want to enjoy myself as a human being."

All the same, one must be careful, as some writers on Sayers have not been, to recognize that she was not unattractive in her youth. Brabazon indicates that if she never qualified as sexually attractive, she had plenty of vitality and appeal, and received offers of marriage. She had a slender neck in those days, and was "long and slim." What she wanted then was "a man to her measure," someone she could fight with and not intimidate. Of course, she found no such man who would have enabled her, she said, to "put a torch to the world." She put a torch to the world by inventing him.

Brabazon is surely right in asserting that it is the creation of Lord Peter Wimsey, and the works in which he appears, through which Sayers has given the greatest pleasure and will be longest remembered. Even in the genre of the detective novel, Sayers's one work without Wimsey, *The Documents in the Case*, for all its virtues, lacks the appeal of the Lord Peter stories: the absence of the moral complexity that Wimsey ensured is sadly felt. High intelligence as a protagonist and the ability to appreciate the inherent complexity of moral decisions are, together with his upper-class manners, what make Lord Peter appealing to so many readers. Intelligent readers like encountering, in fiction, characters as intelligent as themselves, and more erudite.

It has often been said, of course, that Sayers created Lord Peter as the ideal man and then fell in love with him. This, if true, is only partially so. It would be more accurate to say that she created him as an ideal human being, with a feminine sensibility and the male chance for action. Only when he was well established could she, like God, create a woman, Harriet Vane, to bring him comfort, love, and eventually (alas) willing subordination. Harriet Vane has much in common with Sayers, most of all the intelligent woman's inability to find a man worthy of her love. In writing *Gaudy Night*, the novel she had prepared herself all her life to write, Sayers had completed her task of transforming the detective story and embodying her vision of intellectual integrity.

Having done so, she turned, at about fifty, to another career. So, in another fashion, did Virginia Woolf, who, having in *The Waves* written the culminating work of her first art, turned to something more political. (By political, I mean that which hopes to have a palpable effect upon the world and its institutions.) While Woolf and Sayers had little enough in common, they shared the dubious honor of being chosen by Q. D. and F. R. Leavis for passionate attack. Unlike Woolf, Sayers believed the work of her late years to be the destined work of her life: she viewed Wimsey as the financial ground upon which her religious dramas and translations of Dante rested. We may guess that she was wrong in this; her turn to another realm of endeavor more closely resembled the male pattern of a second, less desperate career following success. But all of these around-age-fifty switches have in common the search for a career of generativity rather than stagnation. Some of her readers—myself among them—feel unsympathetic to the tight creed toward which she consecrated her late talents; others welcome her lucid expression of the religious ideas they find adumbrated in the detective novels. But all recognize the important rebirth at the end of life.

Once one has expressed admiration for Brabazon's biography, and regretted the material he could not possibly have included, short of producing a thousand-page book, there remain only a few questionable matters. The first is minor enough: his decision to refer to his subject throughout as "Dorothy." It was the name by which he addressed her during their brief acquaintance; nonetheless, "Sayers" would have been preferable and in keeping with modern usage. (Certain men have a problem here: for example, Gordon Ray, who, throughout his study of Rebecca West and H. G. Wells, calls her Rebecca and him Wells.) One regrets, also, the lack of emphasis on Sayers's friendships with women. Apart from denying that these intense, and intensely intellectual, friendships were lesbian (but Brabazon does not deal with Sayers's great defensiveness on this subject), he explores too little one of the most compelling phenomena of her generation. For the first time, but not for long, young women in England, graduating from the universities, experienced friendship according to the male model, where the intention is to enter the power structure, to become productive, and to encourage and support one another. Brabazon recognizes Sayers as a brilliant correspondent and hopes for an edition of her letters. Certainly her letters to women friends would make a valuable contribution to a general history of those English women who flourished so grandly between the two world wars, in one of feminism's most vibrant periods. Unfortunately, Brabazon devotes too little analysis to Sayers's feminism.

Probably the most glaring flaw in Brabazon's biography is his complacent acceptance of Sayers's anti-Semitism, which, expressed mainly in private letters, need not have been so ardently defended. Brabazon excuses Sayers on the grounds that she knew Jews who refused to "learn the common school code of honour." Leaving aside our knowledge today of where that school code can lead, do we not know that the essence of racial and religious prejudice is to judge a whole group from a few examples of bad behavior? That Sayers actually knew or heard of Jews who behaved badly hardly seems the whole point. Also, Brabazon does not mention Sayers's perfect relations with her publisher, Victor Gollancz, a Jew (though later a convert to Christianity), or the effect upon her of the fact that Cournos was a Jew. Sayers, in fact, disliked the Jewish religion because of its refusal to recognize Jesus as the savior. Sadly, Brabazon, who finds Sayers's tirades against the BBC regrettable because he has worked with the BBC, can only excuse her harshness toward Jews.

Interestingly enough, the American Baptist minister Ralph Hone, author of *Dorothy L. Sayers: A Literary Biography* (1979), is more perceptive on many of these points than Brabazon. He understands Sayers better as a woman and as a feminist and as an anti-Semite. He notices, as Brabazon does not, that Sayers's German governess, whom she kept in touch with and helped after the war, was a Nazi. Hone quotes many of Sayers's feminist views, particularly her wonderful account of the Church's attitude to the story of Martha and Mary. His biography is in no way as complete as Brabazon's, since he did not have access to the family papers, but he has understood Sayers with a certain instinctive sympathy, combined with training in the analysis of literary texts. His biography should be read together with Brabazon's, though there is inevitably much repetition between them. Hone fills in what Brabazon, for reasons of space, excluded—for example, Val Gielgud's report on his interview with Sayers just before her death: "She was positive, as only an inherently shy person can be. And behind a facade occasionally forbidding there was an immense friendliness." Suddenly, one understands so much.

As Sayers grew older and became famous, the necessity of loving one's work became her unremitting watchword. She spoke often of the sense of joy in work that has overmastered one. Certainly this idea is particularly important for those women who must find the courage to resist a lifework that society commends but the soul rejects.

But as Sayers moved into her Christian work, she tended to use the need to love her work as an excuse for avoiding unwelcome tasks. C. S. Lewis wrote to her: "Of course one mustn't do *dishonest* work. But you seem to take as the criterion of honest work the sensible *desire* to write—the itch. That seems to me precious like making 'being in love' the only reason for going on with marriage. In my experience, the *desire* has no constant ratio to the value of the work done." Brabazon suggests that Sayers confused what she ought to do with what she felt like doing. Similarly, today, women who find the courage to pursue their "proper job"—in academia or in the professions or businesses newly opened to women by the efforts of feminists—eschew any support of other women with the excuse that their proper job is being a lawyer, or whatever it might be; thus they avoid their part in the hard and painful task of changing society's restrictions on women.

The importance of much of Sayers's later religious work is indisputable. Her comments on Dante, I have been told, are original and incisive. Her *Mind of the Maker,* as lucid as it is filled with insight, describes her experiences in the writing of detective fiction, to illuminate her analysis of acts of creation by God and by human beings. Her dramas and her translations are, perhaps, less likely to last. As to the Wimsey books, these will endure for the reasons books do endure: because they give pleasure and because, beneath their glittering surface, they question the society they portray. It is easier to be an apologist for a society than a subtle subverter of it.

In 1943, Sayers turned down a Lambeth Degree, a rare honor bestowed by the Archbishop of Canterbury, who offered her a Doctorate of Divinity. Because her letters to the Archbishop have not been released, Brabazon can only guess at her reasons for refusing this great honor, but his guess is a sound one: she was aware of personal sinfulness in her son Anthony's birth, and afraid that the fact of his birth might be ferreted out. We, who now know all the facts, may well decide that it was in her sinfulness, rather than in her preaching, that her true destiny as a woman is revealed.

A Personal Memoir

Dorothy L. Sayers

MICHAEL GILBERT

Since most of my acquaintanceship with Dorothy L. Sayers (from now on to be referred to as Dorothy) stemmed from the Detection Club, I had better start by explaining about this.

There are in England two bodies that concern themselves with crime writers and crime writing. The larger and newer one is the Crime Writers Association (CWA). This corresponds to a similar body in America, the Mystery Writers of America (MWA). Both these bodies are, in many senses of the word, trade unions. In other words, if you possess the necessary qualifications, you can apply for membership and will be admitted.

These qualifications are not onerous. A single crime novel will do it. The Detection Club, on the other hand, really is, and always was, a club. You do not apply to join it. Two existing members put your name forward, the committee considers your qualifications, and if it approves of you will invite you to become a member.

It is important to understand this if one is to appreciate the position Dorothy occupied. The Detection Club is a small, prestigious, self-perpetuating coterie. In its early days it was even smaller, since it was confined to writers of detective stories proper, as opposed to thrillers and spy stories. Dorothy was one of its founders. It started, in 1928, with twenty-six full members, and until the outbreak of war (when the club went into temporary dissolution) only half a dozen others had joined and two had died. Dorothy was its leading light. She held no office until she became president in 1949, but she was in every way its mainspring. She was the promoter of its activities, which included the writing of a number of joint detective novels, a tricky assignment carried out with remarkable success, which added substantially to the funds of the club and helped to pay the rent of its club room, first in Gerrard Street, later in Kingly Street. One of them, *The Floating Admiral*, was republished recently. Even more important, she was the composer of its "ritual." This was an intimidating affair, in which a candidate promised, with his hand on a skull, to adhere to the strict rules of fair play in writing in his whodunits: no clues concealed from the reader, no poisons unknown to science, and (for some obscure reason) no Chinamen.

The only portion of the catechism that I can remember when Michael Innes and I joined in 1949 (we are now its two oldest surviving members) was the final question, asked by Dorothy, with her eye fixed beadily on us—"Do you take *anything* seriously?" To which Michael Innes replied "The Master of Balliol," and I "The President of the Law Society." These replies were apparently judged to be in order by Dorothy, as being in keeping with the solemnity of the occasion.

I emphasize this because it demonstrated to me one important aspect of her character—a mingling of the sort of sophistication in life and living that was appropriate to the creator of Lord Peter Wimsey, with an immature, almost schoolgirlish pleasure in trivialities. One of these was an insistence that she should always be referred to, in writing, as Dorothy L. Sayers. To leave out the middle initial was a deadly insult. I never discovered why and was too timid to ask her.

The late Christianna Brand, who was one of the first members to be elected when the club re-formed in 1946, knew Dorothy well. Dorothy, she said, could be unkind, but was never so to Christianna, who described her as huge and dominating, but friendly (if she liked you) and unpretentious. She reserved her slings and arrows for people who did not take crime writing seriously. Her masculine habits grew more pronounced as she grew older. As they were cleaning the Club Room after a meeting, Christianna would say "Oh Lord, one of the men has left his hat"—only to discover that it was one of Dorothy's many items of male attire. They were very often the last two there, and when everyone had gone home they would sit, one on each side of the gas fire, and talk of life and things. "She would tell me about life at home, which consisted of 'my poor husband, my fool of a woman' (that was her secretary), and the gardener, 'a pig.'"

But even Christianna had to guard her tongue. She recalls an occasion when they were walking together from a committee meeting to the restaurant, "Miss Sayers, huge, walking along in her great gray suit." The talk turned to food, a subject of constant complaint in those days on account of its scarcity. Christianna said, "You know the legend about Buddha, how when all the animals were starving he turned himself into an elephant and threw himself over a cliff so that they might feed upon him." Suddenly she realized that this might be taken as having a personal application to the enormous gray form looming beside her. But Dorothy rarely took offense at personal remarks and roared with laughter.

The first time I met Dorothy was at the annual banquet at the Café Royal at which I was inducted. The monthly dinners were informal get-togethers in Soho, but this was always a special affair, with a distinguished guest and much oratory. On one occasion the members put on a one-act play, *The Case of the French Ambassador's Trousers*, specially written for them by John Dickson Carr. Sherlock Holmes was played by Cyril Hare, who had the exact Sherlockian profile; Doctor Watson by John Rhode; the de-bagged ambassador by Carr himself; whilst Mrs. Hudson was Dorothy, in a red flannel nightgown: an all-star cast.

I came away from this first encounter with two distinct impressions. The first was that Dorothy, though an excellent writer of English prose, was a poor public speaker. Indeed, I think that she probably wrote out her speeches very carefully. They were full of relative clauses and other tricky encumbrances, and Dorothy's delivery did nothing to lighten them. My second impression was that it was very dangerous, so far as Dorothy was concerned, to make fun of the crime novel. The speaker on this occasion was an eminent lawyer. In the course of his speech, which most of the company found highly entertaining, he was rash enough to do just this. Dorothy—though politeness to a guest masked her feelings—was obviously outraged.

But it was at the intimate, private club dinners that Dorothy's character showed itself clearly. I have recorded somewhere an occasion on which she appeared (in the public, not a private dining room) dressed in a sort of rugby football jersey, with a large gunmetal watch pinned across the front of it. At one point in the dinner someone mentioned a fashionable conductor. "He doesn't really conduct," said Dorothy, "he behaves like an intoxicated windmill. Like this." Whereupon she rose to her feet, chanted "da-di-da-dah," and pretended to conduct an orchestra. The sight of that watch, bounding up and down on her ample bosom, seemed to hypnotize the diners at the other tables.

I have often wondered since how much of this outrageous behavior was calculated and how much was simply the residue of a permanent schoolgirl and undergraduate extravagance. In his biography—by a long chalk the better of the first two full-length works that have been written about her—James Brabazon says, "She never made a fool of herself except in her own, particular, calculating way."

So is that the truth—that she indulged in such pantomime in order to be noticed and remembered? I think this might be true, but it is only half the truth. The other half lies in her abiding immaturity, a curious facet of her character when one considers the sophistication of her central character and alter ego, Lord Peter Wimsey, with his musical ability, his taste in vintage wines, and his essentially adult outlook on the motives and characters of people he met. (Dorothy once confessed to me that she could not tell the difference between burgundy and claret, one of many differences between her and her puppet.)

Another difference was that Dorothy was capable, on occasion, of being coarse. Her language was sometimes Rabelaisian. This has been commented on by the dons at Somerville. Dorothy was not ashamed of it. Did she not, at a later period, make a speech called "The Importance of Being Vulgar"?

It was in the after-dinner sessions in the Club Room in Kingly Street that Dorothy really let her hair down. Normally she would react angrily to any criticism of crime writing, but in the company of people who, even if she did not regard them as her equals, were all of them fellow laborers in the same field, she could even, sometimes, tolerate having her leg pulled.

The club at this time was a sort of crime writer's workshop. On one occasion the discussion turned on the difference between the classic detective story, commonly known as a whodunit, and the thriller. The detective story, I ventured to assert, was comparable to the sonnet, being bound in its format by the strict rules that it had to observe. The thriller was the ode, which could adopt any form it chose. I further alleged—and this was bold of me when one considered the ethos of the club—that, having tried my hand at both, I thought the thriller the more difficult of the two.

"You think then," said someone, "that an ode is easy to write." This was a fast ball, which I blocked as well as I could, but surprisingly Dorothy came in on my side. She said that she had never herself attempted a thriller but agreed about its difficulty; to which another member said, "What, never, Dorothy? What about 'The Cave of Ali Baba'?"

If Dorothy had ever been inclined to blush, I think she might have blushed here. The reference was to a short story (the final one in her collection *Lord Peter Views the Body*). It was, as far as I know, her only essay in the thriller *pur sang*, and I suspect that secretly she was rather ashamed of it.

On one occasion only, my exchanges with Dorothy were written rather than verbal, and it is worth referring to, since it has featured in more than one volume on crime writing. It arose out of one of Dorothy's most famous books, *The Nine Tailors*, which, as all addicts will remember, was written around the art and craft of bell ringing. In an article in the Brean *Mystery Writers Handbook* I had been rash enough to suggest that Dorothy knew little about the practice of bell ringing; her knowledge had derived from a casual study of books.

The word *casual* produced a magnificent, and deserved, riposte: "The work I put in on that job was some of the hardest I have ever done. It was spread over two years (during which I had to write *Murder Must Advertise* to keep the wolf from the door) and it included incalculable hours spent in writing out sheets of changes until I could do any method accurately in my head. It was not until after the book was published that I ever even saw bells rung. In the end the experts could only discern three small technical errors. Of this result, I am sinfully proud."

She then added a splendid comment: "It acts as a warning against the type of criticism which asserts that Shakespeare must have been a solicitor's clerk because he could use a few legal terms without making a fool of himself. I doubt whether any critic working on *The Nine Tailors* and *Murder Must Advertise* could decide from internal evidence alone, which of the techniques had been known to me by experience and which by what the schoolmen called 'simple intelligence.' "

This reply demonstrated to me—if demonstration was necessary—the meticulous care that Dorothy exercised over the details of her craft.

Just before Christmas in 1957 my wife and I were up in London buying Christmas cards and met Dorothy on the same errand. Two days later we got a card from her. This didn't normally happen, but perhaps seeing us had put her in mind of it. It was a macabre thing to receive. The *Evening Standard* had announced her death on the previous day.

On January 15 in St. Margaret's Church at Westminster, a crowd of her friends attended the memorial service. Dorothy was credited in the announcement with her M.A. (Oxon) and her D.Litt. (Durham), honors of which she was justly proud.

The lessons were read by Val Gielgud and Judge Gordon Clark (aka Cyril Hare). The panegyric was written by Professor C. S. Lewis and read by Bishop Bell of Chichester. The first hymn was by J. Franck, written in 1670. The second hymn, written by St.

John Damascene in A.D. 750, contained a final verse that has haunted me ever since.

In this may thy poor servant
Her joy eternal find,
Thou callest her. O rest her
Thou Lover of mankind.

The closing hymn was in Latin, "O quanta qualia sunt illa sabbata." It was Peter Abelard's hymn. Five other bishops and representatives of Canterbury took part. Dorothy would have approved highly of all of it.

D. L. S.

An Unsteady Throne?

IAN STUART

When I was ten I started at a school fourteen miles from my home. The school was another mile from the railway station. Classes ended at 3:30, and there was barely sufficient time for me to get my homework—we called it "prep"—together, change my shoes, and run to catch the 3:52 train. If a master kept us a few minutes late, I missed it. And that meant a wait of over an hour for the next one.

In those far-off days, every station of any size boasted separate ladies' and general waiting rooms and a refreshment room. Fortified by a London & North Eastern Railway rock cake, I would spend the time in the general room doing some of my prep or reading a sixpenny Penguin or Crime Club paperback bought at the station bookstall. Thus began a love affair with crime fiction that still endures. I never dreamed then that one day I would write mysteries myself.

I imagine that among the novels of Agatha Christie, John Rhode, and Freeman Wills Crofts, I must have read some of Dorothy L. Sayers's, although I can't remember doing so until several years later. I know that when I did I enjoyed them.

They called Sayers the Queen of Crime. True, it was only her publisher's hype, but there are still people who agree. (Incidentally, we never hear of a king of crime. Not among writers at least. I suppose you could hardly have splashed across a paperback cover the slogan: JOHN DICKSON CARR, KING OF CRIME!)

But if Dorothy Sayers was indeed the queen, I suspect hers was an unsteady throne.

Writers, like boxers or footballers, should always be considered in the context of their time. It is useless to argue whether Louis was a better fighter than Ali, or Vardon a finer golfer than Hogan. Only the very greatest, the Shakespeares and Dickenses, defy the limitations of time. Often, one sees critical assessments all too obviously made with the benefit—and the prejudices—of hindsight. John Buchan, a distinguished and cultured man, has been accused of anti-Semitism, on the basis of passing comments in some of his books. But those books were written more than seventy years ago, and much that offends us today was common usage then. It isn't easy to project oneself back into the writer's time; we are too conditioned by the conventions of our own.

Most of the detective stories of the so-called Golden Age seem dreadfully dated to us now. Many are almost unreadable, turgid and badly written, with cardboard characters and ludicrous plots. The people for whom they were written lived a life as different from ours as theirs was from the Victorians'. Few of them had ever traveled outside their own country, unless it was to endure the horrors of Flanders in the 1914–18 war. They were ignorant of alien ways and contemptuous of foreigners. In detective stories Chinese were invariably sinister, Latins "dagoes," and most others ridiculous or untrustworthy. Dorothy Sayers was an educated, intelligent woman, yet her books contain evidence of those prejudices.

Unlike the other members of the elite quartet—Christie, Marsh, and Allingham—Sayers had finished writing detective stories before the outbreak of war in 1939. Virtually all her novels were produced in the ten years from 1927, and the standards of those days are the yardstick by which they must be judged.

The Golden Age coincided with the Great Depression. People were hungry for escapism, and for many of them the mystery novel was the equivalent of a Fred Astaire/Ginger Rogers or Shirley Temple film, especially if it contained a romantic, aristocratic hero. After all, the majority of the readers of detective stories, as distinct from thrillers, were women. The hero's being unreal didn't matter a hoot. We may sneer now, but he was no more implausible than heroes have been all through the ages—including our own. We need fantasy figures. Women mystery writers understood this and responded, Allingham with Albert Campion and hints of his royal connections, and Marsh with the impeccably upper-class and almost equally improbable Alleyn. Only Agatha Christie resisted the temptation and stuck to her absurd little Belgian.

Lord Peter Wimsey fulfilled all the requirements of the time. He was a duke's son—hence his courtesy title; he wasn't a peer in his own right—and moved in circles Sayers's readers dreamed of but could never aspire to; he was wealthy, brave, handsome, a brilliant sportsman, sophisticated, and experienced with women. He was an expert on everything and given to whistling note perfect complicated passages of Bach. What more could any female reader between the ages of twelve and ninety ask?

A passing thought: where did his wealth come from? Presumably his father's estate was entailed and passed to Gerald, while Wimsey's mother was still alive. One can only hope it was honestly acquired. Oh dear!

Perhaps it is significant that most of his fans are women. Fortunately for the world, men have other, very different fantasy heroes. Not more worthy, in many ways a whole lot worse, but different.

I think it may mean something too that Wimsey is probably more popular nowadays in the United States than in Britain. After all, Americans are more fascinated by titles than the British, and, just as some English men and women see the States as a land of cowboys, gangsters, and Disneyworld, many Americans harbor what to us seem strange ideas about Britain, still believing it to be a country of thatched cottages and castles peopled by indolent lords, quaint yokels, and bobbies on bicycles. Blame Hollywood and the British Tourist Board. Those Americans don't want to read about a modern, technological country, they want to be entertained by handsome lords who have no place in the everyday world. It's why American women writers come to Britain and write ostensibly realistic books that contain about as much reality as a Gilbert and Sullivan opera.

I think that, perhaps, many Americans don't understand the British taste for irony. Americans generally are more literal, more direct, and they accept as fact what is often self-parody, even caricature, in English novels. I once heard a New York academic say that she taught her students that Ngaio Marsh's books gave an accurate picture of the English upper classes. She didn't seem to understand that many of Miss Marsh's people were eccentrics, if not actually caricatures.

In the Golden Age no one cared about glaring inconsistencies, even impossibilities. And Dorothy Sayers—she may have insisted on the middle "L," but when I was a boy no ordinary readers used it—was as guilty as any. Miss Climpson, having served on a jury in *Strong Poison*, proceeds to tell Wimsey the secrets of the jury room, a heinous offense under English law, while in *Clouds of Witness* Parker asks to take over a case in which the chief suspect is his close friend's brother, and is allowed to do so!

Extraordinary methods of murder were in vogue. Nowadays part of the veneer of realism consists of using mundane knives and coshes. At the first meeting of the Crime Writers Association I attended, that good friend and fine writer John Buxton Hilton came up to me and asked in his gruff, friendly tones, "Are you a gun man or a blunt instrument man? I'm a blunt instrument man. If I used guns, I'd get everything wrong." In the thirties no one cared. I recall a book in which the crime was committed by means of a gun fired by an apparatus constructed around a hot water bottle!

Not that Sayers couldn't write well. On a good day she was a far "better" writer than any of the other members of the quartet. It has been said that she made the detective story "respectable" reading for intelligent people, which is a bit hard on Chesterton, Knox, and a good many others. All the same, a respected English author and critic told me that it was only when her husband introduced her to the Wimsey books many years ago that she took crime fiction seriously. Until then she had labeled it all together in her mind as junk.

There is much good writing in *Gaudy Night* and *The Nine Tailors* especially. The first twenty or thirty pages of *Gaudy Night,* describing Harriet Vane's arrival in Oxford and introducing the members of her old college, are first-class (even if there are so many characters that one is forever turning back to see who is who). Some phrases linger in the memory, like "the rough kiss of the sculls on unaccustomed palms." And there are occasional almost Dickensian touches, particularly in *Gaudy Night:* "Only the arrival of two common room scouts to remove the coffee cups and relieve her of the necessity of replying seemed to have saved her from sinking through the floor." The irritating thing is that too often they are followed by woolly, self-indulgent passages. You can't help feeling that the books would have been much better if Sayers had had a firm editor. Certainly some are overlong. *Strong Poison* opens with a long verbatim account of a judge's summing-up in a murder trial; I wonder if any publisher would accept that now. But we are talking of sixty years ago, when readers were less impatient and didn't demand action on every other page.

A good many years ago my family and I were on holiday in southwest Scotland. As the book was set there, I bought a copy of *The Five Red Herrings.* Sad to say, I found much of it almost unreadable. If you want alibis based on timetables, Freeman Wills Crofts handled them much better.

The criticism most often leveled at the Wimsey books is their snobbishness. It jars on modern British sensibilities. But is the criticism fair? The years before 1939 were a snobbish time, particularly in lower-middle-class suburbs. People seeking reassurance and self-esteem erected all sorts of barriers to demonstrate their superiority. These seem laughable now, but they were real enough then.

Many readers took as their role models the upper-class characters portrayed in the books they borrowed so avidly from circulating libraries, not understanding that most of the authors had no closer contact with the aristocracy and knew no more about it than they did themselves. As Colin Watson wrote in *Snobbery with Violence,* their addresses included "precious few manors or granges, but a host of numbered, semidetached houses." Few of them had much to do with "working people" or country dwellers. Their readers accepted stereotyped characters who spoke a peculiar English and were suitably respectful. And, horrible thought, perhaps they snickered a little, their sense of their own superiority pleasantly boosted.

I don't know whether, when she created Wimsey, Dorothy Sayers was deliberately pandering to her prospective readers' tastes—after all, like her alter ego Harriet Vane, she originally wrote mystery novels to make some money—or whether she set out to follow in a tradition of effete heroes in English fiction. The crime writer June Thomson believes he is in a direct line from the knights and their squires of the Middle Ages. That may be going back too far; after all, there was nothing effete about those knights. Rather, perhaps, he is a Don Quixote figure. But most of all he resembles Sir Percy Blakeney and Bertie Wooster, both of whom were extremely popular in the twenties and thirties.

Nevertheless, in the end Wimsey fails. He hasn't the Scarlet Pimpernel's compelling reason for maintaining his foppish pose, and he is fundamentally far more intelligent and serious than Wooster. For all her touches of humor, Sayers hadn't the lightness of touch of a Wodehouse—very few have, of course. But there is a sense of strain about parts of the books. Where Christie's writing strikes one as spontaneous, Sayers gives the impression of careful craftsmanship a little overdone at times. The labored badinage between Wimsey and the insufferably self-absorbed Miss Vane makes very heavy going nowadays—and probably always did.

It is difficult to tell which is the real Wimsey, the affected ass who is also a brilliant detective, or the educated, cultured scholar capable of meeting any intellectual challenge. Perhaps Sayers herself couldn't decide. In *Clouds of Witness* the two sit uneasily side by side and never make a convincing or even very attractive whole. Wimsey's arrival at Grider's Hole isn't so much amusing as absurd. More so the picture of him diving from a great height into a pool at a party in *Murder Must Advertise*. By that time he was a man in his forties.

All crime writers worth their salt are aware of the basic difficulty of their craft, to create seeming reality in what is by its nature unreal. No murder investigation was ever like those described in the classic detective story. There are two ways of dealing with the problem: one is to meet it head-on and create a fantasy world peopled by fantastic characters, the other to paint a thick varnish of reality over everything. Dorothy Sayers fell between those stools; she placed Wimsey, a creature of fantasy, in settings that were overtly realistic.

Nothing places a book in its period more firmly than its settings. This is why, for me, her books have dated so much compared with Agatha Christie's. Mrs. Christie never strove for more than a touch of realism; her books were set in a never-never land bathed in a permanent summer glow, whether it was called St. Mary Mead, Arabia, or the Orient Express, and the real world was always at least a step away. Sayers chose an Oxford women's college, an advertising agency, and an isolated Fenland village and described them in detail. Incidentally, the villagers of Fenchurch St. Paul in *The Nine Tailors* are treated more sympathetically and in greater depth than the country people in her other books, perhaps because the author's father was once a vicar in a similar parish.

And she was wordy. In *Gaudy Night* there is a lengthy description of a publisher's cocktail party that contributes nothing to the story and seems to have been included mainly to tell readers who couldn't know from their own experience what such parties were like. In the same book there are passages of French and Latin, even Greek, while in *Clouds of Witness* a crucial piece of evidence consists of a letter in French that is printed in full, followed by a translation. True, two or three words in the original were vital, but a whole long letter! Again, in one book the French *afficher* is used when an English equivalent would have been both more sensible and more appropriate. But the height of absurdity is reached when Wimsey proposed to Harriet using a Latin question employed in university voting.

These may seem trivial points, but to me they are indicative of a rather unpleasant aspect of the books: Sayers's apparent pandering to her readers' snobbishness, and at the same time flaunting her own superiority. She knew that only a handful of them would understand those passages. It is that which sticks in the gullet: intellectual snobbishness is as offensive as any other sort. And sometimes her efforts at sophistication came unstuck, as when in *Strong Poison* a character speaks admiringly of "a '47 sherry."

The sense of straining for effect is less noticeable in the Montague Egg short stories. This is partly, perhaps, because of the limitations of length, but also, I think, because there is no Wimsey to be portrayed in all his ghastly glamour.

And that is the heart of the problem. Dorothy Sayers's reputation rests on the Wimsey books, and, unthinkable though it may be, wouldn't they have been much better without him?

Nevertheless, though her throne may be rocky and much of the praise ill considered, her books are still read, discussed, and enjoyed sixty years after they were written. How many of us writing now can hope for as much?

Butler, Dabbler, Spy

Jeeves to Wimsey to Bond

WILLIAM F. LOVE

In writing this essay (which started out to be a study of Lord Peter Wimsey), I was struck by the parallels between the novels of Dorothy L. Sayers and those of two other—hugely popular—British writers: P. G. Wodehouse and Ian Fleming. The more deeply I looked into it, the more interested I became. As a result, I will try to show that Sayers is a centerpiece joining the other two.

Wodehouse, Sayers, and Fleming were three of the more popular novelists to come out of Britain in the twentieth century. Wodehouse (pronounced "Woodhouse") had an almost unbelievable longevity as a published author. His first novel, *The Pot Hunters*, was published in 1902; his last (and ninety-sixth), *Aunts Aren't Gentlemen* (U.S. title: *The Cat-Nappers*), in 1974. Dorothy L. Sayers's Lord Peter Wimsey mysteries covered the 1920s and 1930s. And Ian Fleming's James Bond series ranged from 1953 to 1964, ultimately topping the best-seller charts. All three continue to be read widely throughout the English-speaking world. In addition, the BBC productions of the Lord Peter stories have been seen by millions; and every year or so Hollywood brings out another James Bond movie. I believe these writers have more in common than simply their popularity and nationality. I think literary dependency can be traced: from Wodehouse to Sayers; and from Sayers to Fleming. Jeeves to Wimsey to Bond, if you will.

First, Jeeves to Lord Peter. It's a simple matter to prove that Sayers read Wodehouse. No less a Sayers authority than James Sandoe takes it for granted. But we needn't rely on Sandoe: in the early pages of *Murder Must Advertise* Sayers mentions Wodehouse twice.

First, Pym's Publicity's new copy-boy (Lord Peter Wimsey) is compared to Bertie Wooster, one of Wodehouse's major characters: "I think I've seen him," says Miss Meteyard. "Tow-coloured, super-cilious-looking blighter. . . . Cross between Ralph Lynn and Bertie Wooster." (A good indication of Wodehouse's popularity this: Say-ers felt no need to explain to her readers who Bertie Wooster was.) A page later we read about "a bulky, dark youth in spectacles, im-mersed in a novel by P. G. Wodehouse and filching biscuits from a large tin." Obviously, Sayers was conversant with Wodehouse.

But Wodehouse achieved more than mere mention. He clearly left his mark on Sayers. (I suspect he leaves his mark on everyone who reads him. In researching this essay I discovered, to my surprise, clear evidence of dependency on Wodehouse in my own books — despite a thirty-year gap between the last time I read him and the beginning of my writing career.)

As evidence of Wodehouse's influence on Sayers, consider Wim-sey's self-description in *The Nine Tailors*: "I'm a nice wealthy bach-elor. Fairly nice, anyway. And it's fun to be rich. I find it so." Such a self-description would be just as appropriate on the lips of Bertie Wooster.

Or take the way Wimsey occasionally strikes others: "I met [Lord Peter] once at a dog show. He was giving a perfect imitation of the silly-ass-about-town." Later in the same book, another char-acter says, "If anyone asked, 'What is . . . the Oxford manner?' we used to show 'em Wimsey of Balliol. . . . One never failed to find Wimsey of Balliol planted in the centre of the quad and laying down the law with exquisite insolence to somebody. . . . Afterwards, the Americans mostly said, 'My, but isn't he just the perfect English aristocrat?'" Each of these descriptions would fit Bertie Wooster at least as accurately as it fits Wimsey.

Wooster and Wimsey are both bachelors. (Lord Peter's life on the printed page would end shortly after his marriage to Harriet Vane.) Both are hard-drinking, fast-talking party animals with a penchant for finding and losing pretty women. Both have faithful, ingenious butlers. Both, finally, are upper-class, with an unquestioned, albeit unspoken, loyalty to the class system.

But Wimsey moves far beyond Wooster, as the leading character in a series of crime novels should, as opposed to the centerpiece in a set of humorous entertainments. Lord Peter is venturesome, daring, and self-reliant: qualities totally alien to Bertie.

But if Bertie knows nothing of these qualities, that doesn't mean they are absent from Wodehouse's stories. This brings us to the character who is more truly Wimsey's—and therefore Bond's—literary antecedent than Wooster: Wodehouse's supreme creation, Jeeves. Bertie's butler may not be venturesome or daring, but he is supremely self-reliant.

> "Jeeves!"
> "Sir?"
> "I'm sitting on the roof."
> "Very good, sir."
> "Don't say 'Very good.' It's nothing of the kind. The place is alive with swans."
> "I will attend to the matter immediately, sir."
>
> "All is well," I said. "Jeeves is coming."
> "What can he do?"
> I frowned a trifle. The man's tone had been peevish and I didn't like it. "That," I replied with a touch of stiffness, "we cannot say until we see him in action. He may pursue one course, or he may pursue another. But on one thing you can rely with the utmost confidence—Jeeves will find a way . . ."

Jeeves is an expert on fashion, on cuisine, on horse racing, on literature, on politics, and, of course, on *le grand jeu:* he knows precisely the way to a woman's heart.

There are, of course, striking differences as well. Jeeves is primarily concerned with saving his master's onions; Lord Peter is concerned with solving murders. Lord Peter is a master (of Bunter, his butler) and Jeeves a servant. Nonetheless, I maintain, the difference between the characters is far less than the difference between the genres of their stories.

Wodehouse's stories rely on an inverted master-slave relationship as old as Plautus: the servant, for all his social inferiority, is the brains of the pair. Sayers's stories, though they contain an element of irony and self-deprecation (the Egotists' Club, for instance) depend finally on the cleverness of Lord Peter, who, after all, has Jeeves's trick of showing up at exactly the right time and place. (Though Bunter is a faithful servant and a delightful companion, his contributions to Wimsey's crime-fighting tend to be minimal.) Like Jeeves, Lord Peter is omniscient, omnipotent, and always right.

Now to the second point: if Jeeves, the superior servant, is literary antecedent to Lord Peter, the wealthy aristocrat, Lord Peter, with even more justice, can be said to have been the same for Ian Fleming's James Bond.

Not that Bond is either aristocratic or rich. He, first of all, is far from rich — *Moonraker* lists his salary as 1,500 pounds a year taxable, plus 1,000 pounds a year in tax-free income. But (like Jeeves) Bond enjoys elaborate perks, including travel to exotic locales and stopovers at luxury hotels. Furthermore, he never seems to lack for money with which to gamble, occasionally at very high stakes.

As to Bond's place within the British hierarchy of class, he is definitely a commoner. Or is he? Observe him on an outing at M.'s prestigious club, the Blades. We find another inverted master-servant relationship in the two men's dining habits: M., the aristocrat, dines on such items as deviled kidney, bacon, peas, and new potatoes — decidedly proletarian fare — while Bond orders smoked salmon, lamb cutlets, asparagus with Hollandaise. Bond, the commoner, has the upper-class tastes his boss lacks. And though he technically takes his orders from M., he is also shown to be the brains as well as the class of the partnership.

Is some of Lord Wimsey in James Bond? I think so, despite the complete lack of reference to Sayers in any of Fleming's biographies.

First of all, take the following description of Wimsey in *Gaudy Night*: "height of the skull; glitter of close-cropped hair . . . minute sickle-shaped scar on the left temple. . . . Faint laughter-lines at the corner of the eye and droop of lid at its outer end. . . . Gleam of gold down on the cheekbone. Wide spring of the nostril . . . an oddly amusing set of features." Compare this passage, in its wealth of minute detail, to the way Ian Fleming frequently describes James Bond. Ironically, the best of these descriptions is in *The Man with the Golden Gun*, in a passage that describes not Bond but the assassin Scaramanga—who looks enough like Bond to be able to impersonate him successfully:

> Age about 35. Height 6 ft. 3 in. Slim and fit. Eyes, light brown. Hair reddish in a crew cut. Long sideburns. Gaunt, sombre face with thick pencil moustache, brownish. Ears very flat to the head. Ambidextrous. Hands very large and powerful and immaculately manicured.

(Note both writers' use of elaborate detail. Wodehouse, by contrast, is extremely sparing in his descriptions. Virtually all we are ever really told of Jeeves's appearance is that he is a "darkish, respectful sort of Johnny.")

Another connection between Lord Peter and James Bond may be seen in the two men's use of cardsharping to foil villains. Lord Peter's behavior in Sayers's short story "The Unprincipled Affair of the Practical Joker" provides a basis for considering similar activities of James Bond.

In the Sayers story, a parasite named Paul Melville has stolen a diamond necklace from Mrs. Ruyslaender. She is unable to bring charges because along with the diamonds he also stole a small portrait with a highly compromising inscription.

Melville likes to play poker. Lord Peter, knowing of Mrs. Ruyslaender's predicament and wishing to help her, engages the thief in a game. During Melville's deal Lord Peter catches him by the arm, and a card falls from Melville's sleeve. Melville protests his innocence—correctly if vainly—because by adroit sleight of hand Lord Peter had planted the incriminating card on him. Having forced the thief into a corner, Wimsey offers him a way out: if he will return the necklace to its rightful owner he will be allowed to slink away.

This idea of cheating a cheater was used by Ian Fleming more than once, first in *Moonraker*. The initial premise of this book (published in 1955) is that a guided missile capable of reaching any capital in Europe has been developed. The missile is being financed privately by the fabulously wealthy Sir Hugo Drax. The British government is worried that Sir Hugo's propensity to cheat at cards might constitute a risk to national security. For his own good as well as for the defense of the realm, Sir Hugo must be stopped. James Bond, of course, is just the man to catch Sir Hugo out.

Bond is a trained cardsharp: he has learned to handle such tricks as how to drop cards from his sleeve—shades of Lord Peter! M., Bond's superior, invites Bond to the Blades Club, where he engages Sir Hugo in a bridge game and relieves him of fifteen thousand pounds.

But this was not Bond's last dustup with a cardsharp. In *Goldfinger,* the book that constitutes the strongest proof for my contention that Ian Fleming drew inspiration from the works of Dorothy L. Sayers, Bond encounters Auric Goldfinger, money launderer for the evil SMERSH organization. At their first meeting, Goldfinger is cheating at a canasta game at a Caribbean resort: he has positioned a woman in a hotel room behind his opponent to observe his hand through binoculars. She then transmits her findings through a radio disguised as Goldfinger's hearing aid. Bond finds the woman, calls Goldfinger's bluff through the radio, and forces him to make restitution to his victim.

But this byplay between Bond and Goldfinger—so reminiscent of that between Wimsey and Melville—is only the beginning. As the book proceeds, Fleming borrows a murder device employed by Sayers in her short story "The Abominable History of the Man with Copper Fingers."

The narrator of that story, Varden, relates an incident that occurred in the home of the fabulously rich sculptor Eric P. Loder, who lived there with his favorite model, Maria Morano. Loder's specialty as a sculptor was silver castings and "chryselephantine" (gold-and-ivory) overlays. Following a period during which Loder and his model were secluded (ostensibly for artistic work), Loder showed Varden a cast-silver Roman couch in the shape of a nude woman.

Shortly thereafter, while Loder was away, Lord Peter came on the scene and pointed out to Varden that the nude was the silvered body of the model. Loder had silver-plated her as punishment for an affair he imagined her to have carried on with Varden, for whom Loder had planned a similar fate. Thanks to Wimsey's intervention, Varden escaped, and Loder tumbled into a vat of his own cyanide solution.

Goldfinger imitates Loder. Goldfinger has a kinky taste for making love to women coated in gold paint. He leaves unpainted only a strip along their spines, to allow their skins to breathe. When Jill Masterson, Goldfinger's partner with the binoculars, betrays him with Bond, Goldfinger has her painted—entirely—so that Jill dies coated in gold, just as Maria Morales died coated in silver.

Conclusion: Wodehouse influenced Sayers; Sayers influenced Fleming. Jeeves to Wimsey to Bond.

What drove these three popular authors to write? Similarities can be found. According to Paul Gallico, Ian Fleming originally wrote *Casino Royale* as an escape from the "terrifying" prospect of matrimony. As to Wodehouse, reading between the lines of his biographies, we see the lonely child, Plum, passed from boarding school to distant relative, happy only in an imaginary world of comfort and security. These two authors created their own worlds: Wodehouse, a world of comfort and security; Fleming, one of danger and intrigue.

When we ponder Dorothy L. Sayers's career as a scholar and her less than ideal marriage, we may see a certain similarity to Fleming's escape into a world of danger and excitement. Her project, indeed, seems to be encoded in the very name of her hero. Lord Peter is, indeed, an expression of Sayers's *whimsy*.

We are fortunate to have Sayers's own words to guide us, for the following quotation has the ring of a deeply personal sentiment, for all the irony in the second sentence: "Mysteries . . . comfort [a person] by subtly persuading that life is a mystery which death will solve, and whose horrors will pass away as a tale that is told. Or is it pure perversity?" This snippet suggests that Sayers found life a horror; a horror her mystery writing may have mitigated.

A number of critics believe that Sayers, whether knowingly or not, created Lord Peter Wimsey as her beau ideal: the ideal man she could never find in real life. In this connection a line in *Have His Carcase* is revealing: Harriet [Vane] felt she had never fully appreciated the superb nonchalance of her literary offspring." For "Harriet" might we not read "Dorothy"?

Finally, how does Sayers rank as a writer against these other two giants of English literature? I concede she cannot be put in their class when it comes to name recognition of their major characters. "Jeeves" and "James Bond" have become synonymous, among English-speaking people everywhere, for "the proper English butler" and "the quintessential British spy." "Lord Peter Wimsey," resonate though it will for mystery-lovers, is not as recognizable to the public at large.

But popularity is not synonymous with quality; and it is with the quality of the writing I am here concerned. Comparing Sayers with Wodehouse is extremely difficult, since their genres are so different. Wodehouse, it must be said, was a master stylist. Making allowance for the firm and constant placement of his tongue within his cheek, his dialogue and descriptive passages rank high among the masters of the language. If readers are unfamiliar with him, I respectfully suggest they reread the brief passage of dialogue quoted earlier in this paper. The reader whose funny bone is not tickled by that passage is not the Wodehouse type.

In my opinion, Sayers is the finer writer of the two, but I can respect those of the opposite persuasion. What I will not countenance is the opinion that Fleming was Sayers's equal as a writer.

In his preface to the anthology *Gilt-Edged Bonds*, writer Paul Gallico expressed the view that Fleming was a "master of detail." Gallico could not have been more wrong. Fleming's genius lay in expressing certain broad tendencies in the politics and public rhetoric of his day, not in careful craftsmanship. He was a boxer, not a chess player. He didn't write "so that he who reads might run"; rather, he wrote while he ran! Evidence of Fleming's haste can be found throughout his books in numerous errors and inconsistencies.

First, compare James Bond's pharmacology (an important area of his expertise) to Sayers's careful research. His is frequently faulty. In *Moonraker*, in which Bond stirs a dose of Benzedrine into his champagne: " 'It doesn't taste,' said Bond, 'and the champagne is excellent.' " In fact, Benzedrine has an appalling taste, rather like quinine mixed with insecticide. The *Encyclopaedia Britannica* calls it "very bitter and numbing." But Bond doesn't find it so. Nor does the Benzedrine set him off the dinner he is in the process of eating—lamb cutlets with all the trimmings—despite the fact that one of Benzedrine's principal uses is as an appetite *suppressant*.

Bond's understanding of marijuana is even weaker. Later in the same book, he learns of a new Japanese narcotic, addiction to which, "as in the case of marijuana . . . begins with one 'shot.' " [!] And as *Goldfinger* opens, Bond reminisces about a Mexican assassin with pupils tightly *constricted* from the deadly marijuana. [!!] Unfortunately for Fleming, he was writing just prior to a veritable explosion of marijuana information. Had his career been delayed a few years he might have been spared howlers like these.

Bond's French (unlike Sayers's) is little better than his pharmacology: "It was eight o'clock. The Enzian, firewater distilled from gentian that is responsible for Switzerland's chronic alcoholism, was beginning to warm Bond's stomach and melt his tensions. He ordered another double and with it a choucroute and a carafe of Fondant." Leaving aside the imputation that the Swiss are a nation of chronic alcoholics (I more often hear them referred to as workaholics!), Bond has made a rather odd selection from the menu: a *choucroute* is an order of sauerkraut. I presume Bond meant to order a *cassecroute*, or snack (usually some variation on a grilled ham-and-cheese sandwich).

Arithmetic is another chink in the Fleming armor. Consider the incident wherein Leiter complains of receiving short measure from a bartender in his martini. He complains of the large olive, the false bottom in the glass, then notes, " 'One bottle of Gordon's gin contains sixteen true measures—double measures, that is, the only ones I drink. Cut the gin with three ounces of water and that makes it up to twenty-two. . . .' "

Three ounces equal six double measures? Mr. Leiter had shorted himself long before any bartenders had the opportunity to do so.

Not that Ian Fleming can't write. Passages like "a bustle of waiters round their table" or "leashed in by the velvet claw of the front disks, the engine muttered its protest with a mild back-popple from the twin exhausts" show an expertise in the use of vivid metaphors.

I believe Fleming's weakness (and his popularity?) stems from that fact that he eschewed detail work in favor of painting in broad strokes, mythologizing the 1950s and early 1960s, when the headlines were filled with stories of international intrigue.

Double agents Fuchs, Burgess, Philby, Blunt, and Maclean had compromised MI5 (Military Intelligence 5) and even the palace (Anthony Blunt was art historian to the queen). Worse yet, George Blake, imprisoned for fingering forty-two British agents assassinated by the KGB, managed a daring escape from Wormwood Scrubs and was in Moscow almost before his guards knew he was gone. Then in 1963 the John Profumo/Christine Keeler scandal brought down the government.

The British public, frustrated and angered by such blunders and incompetence, needed a distraction. Enter the superhero: ever-competent, never-blundering James Bond.

The Christine Keeler affair is a case in point. It had all the elements of a James Bond story—beautiful women, fantastic wealth, global power, international intrigue: all that's missing is James Bond himself. But compare the Christine Keeler story to a James Bond novel and one begins to see most clearly Ian Fleming's process of mythologization. His purpose was not to analyze or criticize events but to make them larger than life.

Keeler, only nineteen at the time of the Profumo affair, went to prison for two years on rather dubious charges, and lives today in public housing. For James Bond also, beautiful women are expendable, but their ruin is accomplished spectacularly: they are gilded, zapped, shot, stabbed, or exploded; not railroaded—and always in the vital interests of the realm, never for such tawdry, real-life motives as selling newspapers or winning an election.

Fleming's lack of irony is, in fact, characteristic of all his writing. SMERSH, "Smiert Spionam" (= "death to spies"), is described as "the Soviet organization of vengeance and death." Bond himself has a "license to kill." M. (and Bond) react with an outrage completely out of proportion (compared to the matter at hand—the construction of the Moonraker rocket) when they learn of Drax's ungentlemanly cardsharping. And although Bond himself doesn't indulge in racial stereotyping, he accepts such stereotyping without question, as when he is told that Koreans "are the cruellest, most ruthless people in the world," or that Jamaican "Chigroes" (of mixed African and Chinese ancestry) "have inherited some of the Chinese intelligence and most of the Negroes' vices." Fleming's lack of irony, like his carelessness with details, is characteristic of his emphasis on myth.

Sayers's books are much more interesting. Her background is realistic, her characters are three-dimensional, her sense of evil realistic and true to life, her research far more exhaustive than Fleming's.

No better example could be given than the extensive and careful study that went into the descriptions of the ancient art of change ringing in *The Nine Tailors*. This novel has received much praise—some of it from experts in the field—for the accuracy and thoroughness of those descriptions.

Next, I would also call attention to the meticulously plotted and, within the context of the plot, important time sequences in *The Five Red Herrings*. One cannot read that book without being struck by the care with which Ms. Sayers handles those sequences.

As to her overall abilities as a prose stylist, we should start with a concession. She was capable of self-indulgence. Witness the extreme length of *Have His Carcase*, which Sayers can fairly be accused of padding. I personally find none of the Wimsey books tedious, but *Have His Carcase* is not the first, or even the second, book I'd recommend to a budding Sayers enthusiast.

Nonetheless, if Sayers wasn't perfect, she was still a very fine

writer, and capable of some bravura turns. The following mono-
logue (from *The Nine Tailors*) is evidence of an ear finely attuned to
the nuances of local dialect. The speaker is the gravedigger Harry
Gotobed telling how he and his son came upon a corpse in a grave
where it had no business being.

> "Dick drives his spade down a good spit, and he says to me, 'Dad,'
> he says, 'there's something in here.' And I says to him, 'What's that?'
> I says, 'what do you mean? Something in here?' and then I strikes
> my spade hard down and I feels something sort of between hard and
> soft, like, and I says, 'Dick,' I says, 'that's a funny thing, there *is*
> something here.' So I says, 'Go careful, my boy,' I says, 'because it
> feels funny-like to me,' I says, 'that's a boot, that is.' . . . So we clears
> away very careful, and at last we sees him plain. And I says, 'Dick, I
> don't know who he is nor yet how he got here, but he didn't ought to
> be here.' "

Another delightful passage, of a totally different type, is the description of Wimsey's heroics in the cricket match in *Murder Must
Advertise*.

> Mr. Simmonds' third delivery rose wickedly from a patch of bare
> earth and smote [Wimsey] violently upon the elbow.
> Nothing makes a man see red like a sharp rap over the funny bone,
> and it was at this moment that [Wimsey] suddenly and regrettably
> forgot himself. . . . The next ball was another of Simmonds' murder-
> ous short-pitched bumpers, and Lord Peter Wimsey, opening up
> wrathful shoulders, strode out of his crease like the spirit of ven-
> geance and whacked it to the wide. . . .
> Mr. Simmonds . . . was replaced by a gentleman who was known
> as "Spinner." Wimsey received him with enthusiasm . . . till Broth-
> erhood's captain moved up his fieldsmen and concentrated them
> about the off-side of the wicket. Wimsey looked at this grouping with
> an indulgent smile, and placed the next six balls consistently and
> successfully to leg. When, in despair, they drew a close net of fielders
> all round him, he drove everything that was drivable straight down
> the pitch.

If Sayers was the better writer, how then account for Fleming's
greater popularity? The sensationalism of his stories could be part

of the reason, as well as the public's known proclivity for soft-core porn. But I think the primary reason is the power of myth and Fleming's ability to tap into it. Sayers's type of book is aimed at a smaller, more select audience. Jeeves, Lord Peter, James Bond: no one would ever confuse them, but I hope I've shown that they (and their authors) have more in common than meets the eye.

Acknowledgments and sincerest gratitude to Mr. B. C. Lamb for his insights and assistance.

Gaudy Night

Quintessential Sayers

CAROLYN G. HART

Gaudy Night remains—more than fifty-five years after its publication—one of the most unusual mysteries ever written, and, to my mind, it is not only the greatest achievement of Dorothy L. Sayers as a mystery writer but also the most personally revealing book she ever wrote.

Gaudy Night's first departure from mystery novel norms is in its elegance of language. I don't believe there has ever been another mystery writer with Sayers's pyrotechnic felicity with words.

There are many examples of compelling writing in *Gaudy Night*: Sayers's descriptions of Oxford with the students gone, of rowing on the Cher, of the beginning of summer term, of the great solace to be found in scholarship. But, true to the canons of the mystery, Sayers's elegance of expression is never a posturing for show. Her graceful descriptions fulfill their essential function: not a word is included that does not contribute either to setting, to providing requisite information, or to delineating character. Sayers was determined to create a real world. She did it by describing a particular world with utter grace.

So, while *Gaudy Night* is simply Sayers writing as only she could, it differs also from the ordinary mystery in its erudition, in the complexity of its characterizations, and in its passionate espousal of an intellectual theme.

The erudition is there on almost every page—easy references to philosophy, to poetry, to history. But Sayers's erudition never obtrudes; it is the natural manner of speaking and thinking on the part of the novel's principals. Harriet Vane and Lord Peter Wimsey represent the kind of intellectuals Dorothy L. Sayers knew and enjoyed in her everyday life. Their response to all events is enriched by their knowledge of history and poetry and languages, and their knowledge adds texture and resonance to their every utterance. These are people to whom quotations are a way of life, a means of sharing thought and emotion.

But it isn't only in the relations between Harriet Vane and Lord Peter that this is the norm. All of the conversations among this novel's participants intrigue and fascinate, elucidate and mystify, entertain and rebuke, inform and obscure. These conversations give the readers a detailed, realistic, enormously fascinating portrayal of a particular kind of people at a particular moment in history. Sayers insisted that the novel of manners could be wedded to the mystery novel, and *Gaudy Night* proves her thesis.

Much has been made of Sayers's effect on the writing of mystery novels. This can hardly be overstated. The idea of fully exploring human emotion and thought within the framework of a mystery began with Sayers, and her legacy continues today in the works of many authors, especially Amanda Cross, Nancy Pickard, and Sharyn McCrumb. These wonderful writers of today have given us novels of manners within mysteries, a very different matter from the puzzle mystery of Arthur Conan Doyle and the romantic quest mystery of the American private eye genre. And it is Dorothy L. Sayers who led the way.

In *Gaudy Night* Sayers takes a fairly simple story: novelist Harriet Vane returns to the reunion at her college, Shrewsbury, in Oxford, and, to her surprise, learns that unhappiness and ugliness have invaded the sacred vale of academe with poison pen letters and general mischievous destruction of papers and books. The college authorities are disturbed, of course, by this visitation of ill feeling and ask Harriet's advice. There is a strong wish to hide this outburst from the rest of the university, if at all possible, because, at that time, women's colleges were still viewed with suspicion and, by some, with dislike. Harriet tries to discover what she can but is unable to identify the culprit. She returns to her London apartment and soon receives a letter from Shrewsbury, indicating the trouble is continuing and prevailing upon Harriet to offer her good offices. Harriet agrees and returns to Oxford. More episodes occur. Fear grows among the dons that one of the scholars has become unbalanced. Harriet becomes concerned that the perpetrator may move from vandalism to violence, and she tries to get in touch with Lord Peter Wimsey, who is abroad on government business. Wimsey does come to Oxford. There is an attack upon Harriet, which, however, is felt to be aimed at a Miss de Vine. The sense of urgency grows. Lord Peter and Harriet do ultimately unmask the perpetrator.

This simple retelling of the bare bones of plot can in no way suggest the complexity and fascination of *Gaudy Night*, and the questions of ethics and values that it contains. For this is a book about fully realized characters deeply involved in the life of the mind.

Sayers excelled in the creation of vivid characters. Who has read *Gaudy Night* who doesn't recall so many faces and voices and distinct personalities? There is the scholarly commitment of dear, lovable Miss Lydgate ("Oh dear, just a moment, perhaps one more revision of the footnote . . ."), the even temper and judicious temperament of the warden, the rapier-swift mind of Miss de Vine, the callow infatuation of Mr. Pomfret, the sturdy devotion of Padgett, and, of course, always and evermore, the characters who matter the most, who hold the reader in thrall—struggling Harriet, who cannot reconcile mind and body, and patient Lord Peter, who understands only too well yet refuses ever to take any advantage.

It is with Harriet and Lord Peter that Sayers enjoys her greatest triumph, offering to the reader two fully human, complex, imaginative beings who are trying with desperate honesty to forge a balance that will enslave neither.

Perhaps one of the most telling moments in the novel comes at the very end as Peter once again renews his proposal of marriage. But this time, he couches the request in the language used at Oxford graduations. Peter asks in Latin, "Does it please you, Lady Master?" and she replies that it does. So even at this moment, Sayers refines a moment of emotion into a response of the intellect.

Yet despite its serious theme, *Gaudy Night* reverberates with humor: Cattermole's hangdog hangover, the not-quite-penitent prattle of Lord Saint-George, and, of course, certain to delight all writers, Harriet's acerbic view of a literary cocktail party. Sayers loved to laugh. She combined a formidable intellect with a robust humor.

Gaudy Night has long been lauded as the first feminist mystery novel. Certainly it celebrates women as thinking beings equal to achieving any goals they set and points out the obstacles women faced. Women had studied at Oxford since 1870, but Sayers was one of the first generation to be granted a university degree, and she believed fervently that women not only were capable of excelling in the world at large but that they should be free to do so. So yes, *Gaudy Night* is a wonderful feminist novel that still speaks to women today. Especially welcome to today's readers is Lord Peter's disclaimer of men's having any right at all to approve or disapprove of Shrewsbury. Lord Peter here becomes our first male hero to see women truly as equals.

Sayers's cry for equality makes *Gaudy Night*, in the eyes of current women writers, fully modern, fully integrated into the contemporary world of the mystery. In my view, it is the unstated but implicit feminism of mysteries by today's women writers that has captured readers' hearts and minds and made mysteries by women enormously important in the marketplace.

American women still earn less than men with comparable jobs. They are promoted at a slower rate. And, for many years, there was little market for mysteries by American women. The market at that time belonged to the American mystery—i.e., the Dashiell Hammett romantic quest mystery written by males with male protagonists—and to the traditional mysteries written by British women. But beginning with Marcia Muller's first Sharon McCone mystery in 1978, a transformation began. Today, mysteries by American women, both the romantic quest with women protagonists and the traditional mystery in an American voice with women protagonists, have remade the face of mystery selling. Books by American women mystery writers are fabulously successful, and they are books which celebrate both the independence and freedom of American women and the reality of the lives they lead. Both of these qualities go right back to *Gaudy Night*.

So, yes, *Gaudy Night* is a wonderful feminist mystery and still an inspiration to women writing today. But I do not see feminism as the heart and soul of *Gaudy Night*. Important, integral, visionary, but not the heart and soul of that novel.

The heart and soul of *Gaudy Night* is the importance of scholarship, which is, when all is said and done, the impartial search for truth.

Truth. That is Sayers's message.

Truth must be served—in scholarship, in human relations, in living a life.

Sayers makes her point so clearly:

When Harriet first returns to Shrewsbury, she wishes she could once again immerse herself in scholarship because, she realizes, it is only the putting together of pieces of truth that ultimately matters. Not the pain and passions of life, but the garnering of facts, the rooting down through misconceptions and evasions and illusions to reality.

In the hall at dinner that first night after her return, Harriet thrills to the sense of a corporate entity devoted solely to the integrity of the mind. There is a recognition here of connectedness and how uplifting it is to be a part of a concerted, combined effort to seek truth.

In a conversation with Miss de Vine, Harriet exults over the enormous surge of excitement and delight a writer experiences when a written passage is perfect. (Later in her life, Sayers saw work—whatever it might be for each individual—as the proper offering to God. Sayers believed that creativity was what God and man had in common, and the author's joy in a successful effort was the joy of a creator.)

After returning from a vigorous row on the river, Harriet sits in her study and recaptures the excitement she'd felt as an undergraduate in the exercise of thought.

Harriet and Peter mourn together for those wonderful long-ago days when they had work that filled them with joy, the work of the intellect, the search for truth.

Just before they meet with the suspects in the Senior Common Room in the finale of their search for the poison pen malefactor, Peter reveals to Harriet that it is her insistence—always—upon the unvarnished truth that he values most highly in her.

In passage after passage, the point is made: all that matters in life is truth, and perhaps the finest truth of all is the dispassionate product of a scholar's mind.

That this was not only the major theme of *Gaudy Night* but a governing passion in Sayers's life is easily proven. Her last full-length detective fiction, *Busman's Honeymoon,* was published in 1937. Other than some short pieces featuring Wimsey in *The Spectator* in support of the war effort, Sayers devoted herself for the remainder of her life to religious writing and, ultimately, to the translation of Dante. Throughout her life she had authored scholarly works and poetry, and written religious plays both for stage and radio in the late thirties and early forties; these became the focus of all her efforts and energies after *Busman's Honeymoon.*

Her final passion was to translate Dante. I love the picture one has of Sayers concentrating on that work despite the rain of German V-2 rockets. It was, in fact, during an air raid that she snatched up a copy of Dante and fled with it to the cellar. By the time the all clear sounded, she was fascinated by Dante and had found the work that would consume her efforts from that time forward.

I have to feel that, despite the war, despite any personal tribulation she faced, these final years must have been the happiest ones for Dorothy L. Sayers. She was at work, work she valued, seeking ultimate truth, immersed in the selfless seeking-out of knowledge for its own sake, living out her belief that, above all else, all that really mattered in this world of pain and passion was Truth.

The Marriage of True Minds

B. J. RAHN

Dorothy L. Sayers was the first author to employ the detective story to write about important feminist issues. She used crime fiction to try to change rigid attitudes toward sexual roles. She advocated sexual equality in professional life, equality of sexual freedom, and female autonomy within marriage. Moreover, she provided insight into the vast literary potential of the whodunit. She was the first woman to write a detective novel that deserves to be regarded as serious literature. By implementing the full panoply of literary technique in her detective novels, Sayers more than any other writer of the Golden Age prepared the way for the transformation of the mystery story into the crime novel. In a series of four novels using the developing relationship between Harriet Vane and Lord Peter Wimsey as a vehicle, Sayers employed the detective story to explore female integrity, independence, and identity.

Harriet and Peter first meet in *Strong Poison* when she is on trial for having murdered her lover, Philip Boyes, by putting arsenic in his coffee. Peter is moved by her tragic dignity while in the dock and by the unflinching honesty of her testimony. She does not seek to obfuscate or excuse the nature of her relationship with Boyes, even though it flouts social conventions and may prejudice people against her. Realizing her commitment to the truth, Peter believes her when she says that she is innocent. (He later tells her in *Gaudy*

Night that he loves her for her honesty.) When the jury cannot reach a unanimous verdict, the judge orders that the case be retried. In the thirty days before the new trial, Peter launches a successful investigation to prove Harriet's innocence by identifying the real murderer and finding evidence of his guilt. Throughout the course of the narrative, he has only four short private conversations with her during which he proposes marriage and declares his passion—in that order—while posing queries and reporting progress on the case. His sleuthing seems to be more keenly motivated by a personal attraction to Harriet and by what he calls "the fun of it" than by a desire for abstract justice. Nonetheless, Harriet is completely exonerated at the end of the novel and finds herself in the position of owing him her life.

Through the behavior of the court toward Harriet, Sayers exposes the unfair double standard by which men and women are judged in sexual matters. The prosecution obviously regards Boyes's murder as a crime of passion, and the judge in his summation to the jury condemns sexual freedom. He acknowledges that Boyes persuaded Harriet to live with him "in an irregular manner" by convincing her that he was "conscientiously opposed to any formal marriage." Allowing that Boyes was an attractive man whom any woman might have found it difficult to resist, the judge nevertheless goes on to discredit "free love" as merely an "ordinary vulgar act of misbehavior." He even suggests that Harriet is a person of "unstable moral character."

Furthermore, he also rejects the defending counsel's attempt to gain sympathy for her position by pointing out the double standard governing men's and women's sexual behavior. The judge deprecates the idea that "the woman always has to pay more heavily than the man" for unorthodox sexual arrangements. After reviewing rather skeptically Harriet's explanation of her rejection of Boyes's belated marriage proposal—"that she was angry with Boyes because, after persuading her against her will to adopt his principles of conduct, he then renounced those principles and so . . . 'made a fool of her' "—the judge in his final remarks states:

"I am bound to tell you that murders are very often committed for what seem to be most inadequate motives. . . . Especially where the parties are husband and wife, or have lived together as husband and wife, there are likely to be passionate feelings which may tend to crimes of violence in persons with inadequate moral standards and of unbalanced mind."

The judge quite clearly believes that any woman who consents to live with a man out of wedlock is a creature of such uncontrollable passions and such mental instability as to be capable of the most violent crimes. Thus Harriet is unfairly and irrationally victimized for exercising sexual liberty. (One cannot help but be reminded of F. Tennyson Jesse's *A Pin for the Peep Show*, wherein a woman on trial for murder is condemned because of her sexual infidelity rather than actual complicity in the crime). Sayers addresses the question of sexual freedom for women again in *Gaudy Night* when Harriet asks herself whether what she has done is worse than what thousands of others have done, and when she considers solving the conflict of head and heart by engaging in discreet sexual affairs as men do.

Sayers also seeks to establish equality within the heterosexual relationship by condemning Harriet's subservient relationship with Boyes and offering an alternative model in her relationship with Peter. During an interview, Peter asks Harriet why she got involved with Boyes. Harriet admits a combination of motives—fondness, pity, physical attraction, and weakness—led her to give in to Boyes's demands. But she is indignant when Peter inquires if they were friends:

"No . . . Philip wasn't the sort of man to make a friend of a woman. He wanted devotion. I gave him that. I did, you know. But I couldn't stand being made a fool of. I couldn't stand being put on probation, like an office-boy, to see if I was good enough to be condescended to. I quite thought he was honest when he said he didn't believe in marriage—and then it turned out that it was a test, to see whether my devotion was abject enough. Well, it wasn't. I didn't like having matrimony offered as a bad-conduct prize. . . . Well, there it is. I thought Philip had made both himself and me ridiculous, and the minute I saw that—well, the whole thing simply shut down—flop!"

Thus Harriet shows moral integrity, self-respect, and independence in leaving Boyes. And Sayers creates a female character whose humanity stretches beyond sexual stereotyping.

Through the character of Wimsey, Sayers offers a model of enlightened male behavior. Wimsey desires intellectual companionship in a mate and expects equality in a partner. In a rather jejune fashion he announces that he would like to marry Harriet, because "I'd like somebody I could talk sensibly to, who would make life interesting." When Harriet suggests that he would not want a wife who wrote detective novels, Wimsey protests that indeed he would. Thus Sayers provides a male role model who welcomes independent interests in a wife. Wimsey then registers his rejection of male dominance when he congratulates Harriet on her repudiation of Boyes's male-supremacist attitude with a derisive allusion to Adam and Eve in Milton's *Paradise Lost:* "He for God only, she for God in him." And almost immediately thereafter, Peter endorses a single standard for judging sexual behavior despite Harriet's doubts about his family's approval.

> "But, by the way, you're bearing in mind, aren't you, that I've had a lover?"
> "Oh, yes. So have I, if it comes to that. In fact, several. It's the sort of thing that might happen to anybody."

Peter reveals his essential fair-mindedness when they discuss sexual jealousy. After Peter confesses that he is jealous of Boyes, Harriet states, "You would go on imagining things in spite of yourself. You couldn't give me a square deal. No man ever does." He tries to even things up by inviting her to be jealous of his former lovers. Moreover, he indicates his antipathy for sexual dependency ("I loathe being helped and understood") and further establishes equality as he reveals himself capable of being wounded by a lover as Harriet has been.

Harriet demonstrates independence and integrity throughout the novel, but her self-respect is damaged by having her professional achievements deprecated and her unconventional personal life examined in public and held up to censure in a court of law. She refuses to marry Peter because it would be unfair to him but offers unenthusiastically to live with him. Her self-esteem is so low that she cannot believe anyone would offer her an honorable proposal of marriage or that she could escape public disapprobation for accepting it. Moreover, she is so disillusioned that she cannot believe any man trustworthy—even the man who has just saved her life. And of course she is so exhausted by the ordeal of nearly being falsely convicted of murder that she needs time to recuperate. This is not a moment for making new personal commitments. Harriet is experiencing an identity crisis and needs to rebuild her faith in herself as well as her fellow man.

The second novel in this series, *Have His Carcase*, takes place eighteen months later. Harriet discovers the body of a young man with his throat cut while she is on holiday on the Dorset coast. Although she knows better than to disturb the body, she very sensibly takes photographs of the corpse and, before leaving to notify the police, picks up loose objects that might be material evidence. Because of inadvertent delays in reporting the crime, the body is washed away by the tide before the police can examine it, and Harriet finds herself a suspect in a murder case once again. When a Fleet Street reporter learns about the crime, he notifies Peter, who travels to Dorset immediately in order to help Harriet and assist the police with their inquiries. Harriet is thus placed in the same situation all over again and registers her resentment over her dependent position. In this book, Sayers focuses on problems that result from inequality in a relationship.

During this investigation, Peter shows respect for Harriet by taking her seriously and working with her on equal terms. Although Peter solves the puzzle, Harriet makes important contributions to the investigation. She functions well as his investigative partner. But her resentment of her obligation to Peter flashes out in savage anger. She says that his chivalry humiliates her: "You think if you go on long enough I ought to be touched and softened. Well, you're mistaken, that's all. I suppose any man thinks he's only got to go on being superior and any woman will come tumbling into his arms. It's disgusting." Peter protests that the situation places unfair constraints upon him also: "Do you think it's pleasant for any man who feels about a woman as I do about you, to have to fight his way along under this detestable burden of gratitude?" He complains that the situation has forced him to play the buffoon, that circumstances have robbed him of the common man's right to be serious about his passions. Peter recognizes her conflict, but he wants her to behave in a mature fashion, which her vulnerability renders her incapable of.

> "I do understand. I know you don't want either to give or to take. You've tried being the giver, and you've found that the giver is always fooled. And you won't be the taker, because that's very difficult, and because you know that the taker always ends up by hating the giver. You don't want ever again to have to depend for happiness on another person."
> "That's true. That's the truest thing you've ever said."
> "All right. I can respect that. Only you've got to play the game. Don't force an emotional situation and then blame me."

Peter also invites her to "fight it out on equal terms" and enjoy the skirmish.

At the end of the novel, she agrees to return with Peter to London. The expression of her acceptance is couched in a commonplace but significant remark: "We'll go home." The first-person plural pronoun is echoed by Peter: "Right-ho! We'll go home. We'll dine in Piccadilly." The casual use of the "we" indicates a new accord in their relationship and a new sense of partnership. Harriet begins the process of recovery in this second novel. She functions well on her own, independent of Wimsey, and she functions efficiently with him. She begins to trust and accept him and to show signs of attraction to him.

Gaudy Night takes place eighteen months after the case at Wilvercombe and three years after Harriet and Peter first meet. When despite anxiety over her reception Harriet goes back to Shrewsbury

College in Oxford for a Gaudy (an occasion on which former students return to pay respect to the college), she is welcomed by her former tutors and old friends. Her pleasure is tarnished, however, when she finds an obscene drawing in the college courtyard and later receives a poison pen letter. When because of her previous experience with criminal investigation the dons subsequently invite her to investigate the disturbances caused at the college by the combination poltergeist and poison pen, Harriet accepts. After her efforts prove unsuccessful, she requests help from Peter, who solves the problem with her assistance. During the progress of the investigation, Harriet recovers her sense of self-worth and resolves her conflict with Peter.

In *Gaudy Night* Sayers presents the case for sexual equality in professional life by offering a single standard for judging the intellectual and moral probity of both men and women. She develops the theme of professional equality by presenting the responsible behavior of the women dons in a crisis. As individuals and as a group, the dons evince professional integrity by putting academic honor ahead of personal concerns and by valuing abstract truth above self-interest. They are serious, competent scholars and teachers who are committed to both learning and teaching. They are as competent and as sane as male dons. Moreover, they display ethical behavior as well as intelligence; they show charity in their treatment of dishonest and demented staff members.

Sayers embodies her defense of intellectual women in the central action of the detective plot. She sets up a conflict between the "womanly" woman and the professional woman in which she discredits superstitions concerning the mental stability of celibate women and shows instead the violent irrationality of a sexually experienced traditional woman. The persecution by the poison pen is motivated not by the repressed impulses and starved appetites of soured virginity but by resentment against one of the dons, who exposed an academic fraud perpetrated by the culprit's husband and thus ruined his career. The wife cannot blame her husband for his disgrace and their subsequent suffering because she loves him, so she transfers the blame to his accuser and by extension to all other academic women. She disputes the importance of abstract truth and the value of scholarship as she presents the case for physical and emotional loyalty as the *only* morality for women and would reduce female behavior to an atavistic, uncivilized level. But her obsessive personal devotion produces demented, antisocial behavior.

During the course of the novel Harriet regains her sense of herself as a person and as a woman. She retrieves her self-respect and her self-confidence. Moreover, she learns to integrate the intellectual, emotional, and physical aspects of her complex personality—but not without anguish.

Following her trial, Harriet attempted to rebuild her confidence by pouring herself into her work. She clung to her identity as a successful detective novelist as proof of her worth. In seeking to heal the wounds caused by her involvement with Philip Boyes, she turned to her writing for relief and fulfillment. That is, she used her work to take her mind off her unhappiness, her concrete professional achievements to bolster her ego.

She also utilized it as a defense against the importunities of Peter Wimsey. After their experience in *Have His Carcase*, she went on an extended tour of Europe gathering material for two novels and several short stories. While she was away, she neither heard from nor wrote to Peter. She reckoned that after so long a break in their relations, there would be little difficulty in bringing the friendship to a cool and friendly close. She measured the success of her self-imposed therapy by the calmness with which she observed Peter from a distance at the Ascot races, surrounded by female admirers.

The invitation to the Gaudy imposes the first real test of Harriet's newfound equanimity. Having "broken all her old ties and half the commandments," she is full of trepidation at her reception by dons and old friends alike. Harriet refuses to give in to her fears, but despite her brave resolution, she is guilty of defensive behavior manifested in her choice of "unimpeachably correct" clothing for the weekend events and in her growing nervous tension as she approaches Oxford. She summons courage to face the ordeal of meeting people by reminding herself that past or ensuing events, no matter how sordid, cannot rob her of having achieved the status of Master of Arts—an inalienable place, worthy of reverence. Thus she props up her sagging ego by consciously asserting her identity as a scholar.

During the Gaudy, Harriet gains a further confirmation of her professional vocation following a conversation with Miss de Vine, who tells Harriet how one can know what is important in life.

> "We can only know what things are of overmastering importance when they have overmastered us." Was there anything at all that had stood firm in the midst of her indecisions? Well, yes; she had stuck to her work—and that in the face of what might have seemed overwhelming reasons for abandoning it and doing something different. . . . She had written what she had felt called upon to write; and . . . she had no doubt that the thing itself was the right thing for her. It had overmastered her without her knowledge or notice, and that was the proof of its mastery.

While she is at Shrewsbury, Harriet weighs the pros and cons of the contemplative versus the active life, the academy versus the secular world, celibacy versus marriage, professional versus personal fulfillment. The Gaudy provides a large number of opportunities to observe the success and failure various people have made of their choices. While in Oxford Harriet is able to put her own life in a larger perspective.

> The fact that one had loved and sinned and suffered and escaped death was of far less ultimate moment than a single footnote in a dim academic journal establishing the priority of a manuscript or restoring a lost iota of subscript.

> Learning and literature have a way of outlasting the civilization that made them.

By the time she leaves Oxford, Harriet feels much more secure.

In Harriet's thoughts the Gaudy assumes symbolic significance and functions as a watershed. When she returns to London, she takes stock and realizes that the past is dead, that she has left the horror behind her. "Clinging on, by blind instinct, to the job that had to be done, she had fought her way back to an insecure stability." In addition, the Gaudy has revived an old dream of being a scholar. Still under the spell of Oxford, she wonders whether it is too late "to achieve wholly the clear eye and the untroubled mind." But Harriet's idealized vision of the academic cloister is jeopardized by the attacks of the poison pen. She ponders upon the unhealthy results of denying the flesh to cultivate the life of the mind when women are confined in celibate communities. Her lack of faith in herself is extended to her whole sex.

While she conducts the undercover investigation to identify the poison pen, she exercises her skills as a scholar by helping the English Tutor restore the proofs of a manuscript damaged by the poltergeist. She also undertakes scholarly research of her own concerning Sheridan Le Fanu. In addition, she continues to work on a whodunit. She even strives to rise above genre writing and bring her detective novel closer to mainstream fiction by developing her characters more fully. All of these activities serve to confirm Harriet's sense of herself as a competent professional person.

Harriet also demonstrates integrity by subordinating personal comfort and convenience for the good of the college. "There did come moments when all personal feelings had to be set aside in the interests of public service; and this looked like being one of them." After she agrees to undertake the investigation, she swallows personal insults and eventually even risks her life.

Harriet experiences greater difficulty in rebuilding her sense of herself as an attractive, sexually desirable woman. She has trouble in accepting her own sexual needs and learning to trust a man again. At Oxford, Harriet becomes involved with some undergraduates, notably one Reginald Pomfret, whose friendship serves to restore some of her confidence in herself as an attractive woman.

> She was surprised to find how much Mr. Pomfret's simple-minded proposal had elated her. . . . She had taken it for granted that she could never again attract any man's fancy, except the eccentric fancy of Peter Wimsey. And to him she was, of course, only the creature of his magnanimity.

Harriet's problems of sexual identity are finally resolved when she learns to integrate her intellectual and emotional needs by preserving her autonomy in her relationship with Peter. Sayers thus completes her model of the ideal heterosexual relationship as Harriet and Peter resolve their conflicts. They learn to share weaknesses as well as strengths, to be mutually dependent without sacrificing their individual identities.

When Harriet dines with Peter after the Gaudy, she tells him of several distinguished women scholars who were extinguished by matrimony. Peter offers similar examples of men whose wives' demands stifled their creative talent. These remarks lead to a discussion of the claims of head and heart. Harriet seems inclined to choose between the claims of intellect and emotions, whereas Peter suggests a compromise. Harriet eventually rejects this unnatural polarity of human needs and agrees to marry Peter, but only after overcoming her distrust of male dominance and possessiveness by testing Peter almost to the breaking point.

At first Harriet is afraid to enter into a relationship with Peter because she gave up her independence to Philip Boyes and suffered grievously for it.

> She had tried to believe that there was happiness in surrender. . . . It was not to Philip she had submitted so much as to a theory of living. . . . To subdue one's self to one's own ends might be dangerous, but to subdue one's self to other people's ends was dust and ashes.

She has to learn to trust Peter not to undermine her autonomy. She is very defensive about her dependence and resents owing Peter her life. She admits that she has an inferiority complex and wishes she could have met him on equal terms. Her self-esteem is so dependent on her independence that she cannot even accept trifling gifts from him. Nor can she express gratitude.

Harriet also registers fear of being overwhelmed by Peter's superior intellect and force of personality, as much as by sexual possessiveness. She overcomes her fears only when he demonstrates that he has self-control enough not to try to dominate her, that he really wants an independent, equal partner. Equality involves sharing weaknesses as well as strengths, taking as well as giving. When Peter reveals his weaknesses, Harriet gains more confidence. A series of episodes charts the growing trust in the relationship and discloses its terms. In addition, they both have to respect the other's right to take risks; that is, they learn to abandon protective attitudes. Peter admits Harriet's right to risk her life in serving the college; she accepts his right to take his risks on his missions for the Foreign Office and in marrying her.

After the exposure of the poison pen, Harriet and Peter have a crucial interview on the roof of the Radcliffe Camera overlooking the city. In effect, they make peace and resolve old misunderstandings. Peter apologizes for his selfish insensitivity in urging his addresses on her too soon, but explains that they were born of anxious love, his fear of losing her just after he had found her. He acknowledges his chagrin in realizing she had offered him her body but not her self to settle a debt. Harriet reiterates that her confidence was so low at the time she did not in all conscience feel herself worthy of marriage. He asks that she never insult him again with such an offer. Harriet acquiesces—not only because she has recovered her self-worth but also because now the offer would mean something to her.

He asks for a second chance, that is, for forgiveness for his mistakes, since he has worked so hard to tear down the barriers he was responsible for erecting by his own selfishness and folly. Harriet insists it is she who ought to apologize for her harsh, inconsiderate treatment of him. After all, she owes him her self-respect and her life and wants to offer her gratitude. She can say it without the bitterness she felt earlier. Peter points out that by letting her risk her life, he has given it back to her. He does not want her gratitude, but when he accepts it, all debts are settled; the slate is wiped clean.

This is a most important moment in their relationship, the crucial turning point. They face each other as two completely free, independent, equal human beings. Peter even remarks, "You are free now and for ever, so far as I am concerned. You saw yesterday what personal claims might lead to—though I didn't intend you to see it in quite that brutal way." Again, Peter is both unselfish and honest. Having set her free, he is prepared to let her walk away. But his hope is restored by her confession that she is following his advice in reshaping her novel. It is significant that she has admitted him into the most important area of her life.

The final skirmish in this courtship is fought on Peter's last night in Oxford. At a Bach concert at Balliol Peter again states his definition of an ideal partnership in a musical metaphor.

> "Peter—what did you mean when you said that anybody could
>   have the harmony if they would leave us the counterpoint?"
> "Why," said he . . . "that I like my music polyphonic. If you think
>   I meant anything else, you know what I meant."
> "Polyphonic music takes a lot of playing. You've got to be more
>   than a fiddler. It needs a musician."
> "In this case, two fiddlers—both musicians."
> "I'm not much of a musician, Peter."
> ". . . I admit that Bach isn't a matter of an autocratic virtuoso and
>   a meek accompanist. But do you want to be either?"

Thus Peter registers his preference for two autonomous individuals within the relationship, while Harriet expresses lack of faith in her ability to sustain her part.

After the concert, Peter bravely "faces the music" by stating that he has not asked Harriet to marry him since coming to Oxford because he knew he would have to abide by her answer, and he promises that he will. When he asks the question, Harriet shies away from committing herself by inquiring if her refusal will make him desperately unhappy. He scoffs at such language, and in effect refuses to beg or bully her. By resisting the temptation to put pressure on her, he insists that she make up her own mind—to enter into the relationship or to reject it as a free and equal partner. As predicted by Miss de Vine, he forces her independence upon her. But he generously makes it easy for her to refuse him by couching his proposal in the negative. Perhaps because of this final proof of his respect for her autonomy as well as his need for an equal partner, Harriet is able to take her own courage in hand and accept him.

In the final novel in this series, *Busman's Honeymoon,* described by Sayers as "a love story with detective interruptions," Harriet and Peter discover a corpse in the cellar of their Elizabethan country house. Their honeymoon is interrupted by the efforts of the police to investigate the crime and by various village characters who call at inconvenient times. Most of the material evidence has been unwittingly destroyed before the discovery of the body, so the problem of how and when the murder was committed is difficult to solve. When Peter does reconstruct the crime, the murderer is startled into a confession.

In the interludes between the detective interruptions, Sayers reveals Harriet and Peter trying to live by the principles they espoused in *Gaudy Night.* The investigation takes only two or three days, but the time frame of the novel extends to include the execution of the culprit. The first sign of conflict to mar the happiness of the lovers occurs when Harriet tries to dissuade Peter from communicating to the police information that was given to her in confidence by someone whom she wants to protect. She balks at violating a trust. Peter reminds her of their obligation to the dead man, who cannot seek justice for himself, and to the other suspects whose lives might be ruined.

Peter says, "It's evidence. We can't pick and choose. Whoever suffers, we *must* have the truth. Nothing else matters a damn." Harriet agrees in theory but asks whether Peter has to do the dirty work. He replies, "I have given you the right to ask me that. You married into trouble when you married my work and me. . . . Well, Harriet, we are married now. We are bound. I'm afraid the moment has come when something will have to give way—you, or I—or the bond."

When he sees how upset Harriet is, however, he offers to take her away and forget about the case. Harriet is appalled that he would allow his affection for her to corrupt his integrity and rejects his offer. She refuses to engage in emotional blackmail and insists they fight it out like gentlemen when they disagree.

> "Whatever marriage is, it isn't that. . . . You *must* do what you think right. Promise me that. What I think doesn't matter. I swear it shall never make any difference [to my love for you]."

He took her hand and kissed it gravely.

"Thank you, Harriet. That is love with honour."

They stood so for a moment; both conscious that something had been achieved that was of enormous—of overmastering importance.

Ironically it is Peter's autonomy that is threatened in this crisis, not Harriet's, but she reveals that she is as willing to respect the need for integrity and equality in a partner as she is to claim them for herself.

Harriet's resolution not to interfere with Peter's autonomy is put to a further test when she resists attempting to assuage his guilt and pain at bringing a man to the gallows: "I loathe being helped and understood." She allows him to suffer until he seeks comfort by sharing his misery with her. Peter has to bring himself to accept the role of taker after years of giving. Harriet reminds him that if he had not identified the villain, the court might have convicted the wrong person, as it had almost done in her own case. Sayers leaves the reader with an image of two individuals whose personal identities remain intact within marriage, but who are more fulfilled by sharing strengths and weaknesses in a bond of mutual dependence.

In her generation Sayers's feminist idea of suggesting a professional alternative to marriage as a fulfilling lifestyle for women was radical. But she could not sanction sexual experience outside marriage for her heroine because of the strength of prevailing social mores. Although she attacked the double standard and advocated equality of sexual freedom for women, she backed down from choosing a completely emancipated life for her heroine. Instead, she advocated autonomy for women within marriage. In so doing, she reflects a realistic assessment of what was possible at the time.

Thrones, Dominations

Unfinished Testament to Friendship?

ALZINA STONE DALE

Most of her fans are unaware of the fact that when Dorothy L. Sayers declared that there would be no more "Peter Wimseys," she had among her papers a good-sized chunk of a sequel to *Busman's Honeymoon*. Sayers called it *Thrones, Dominations* because, as she wrote to her good friend and fellow Detection Club member Helen Simpson, she had found not only a title but also a grand motto for the book in Milton's *Paradise Lost*. In her letter to Simpson Sayers insisted that the quotation gave "the whole theme of the book in a nutshell." Sayers also sent Simpson a "thematic structure" of the novel with its plot lines drawn in green (for the Wimseys), red (for the murderer), and purple (for the victim)—"because she liked fooling around with coloured inks."

Helen Simpson wrote back that the novel's plan was "shapely as a new laid egg" and the motto could not be improved upon, adding that the whole diagram would come in handy when Sayers actually wrote the mystery. Simpson discussed several of the characters, such as the rather irritating, self-pitying ex-con father of Rosamund Harwell, but her letter fails to make clear whether she ever read any of the actual manuscript.

Unfortunately, today's readers of the fragment—not having Sayers's colorful diagram—won't find her poetic clue as much help as

Simpson did. Instead they will still wonder what the story is all about and why Sayers never finished it.

Sayers's quotation from Milton, which appears on the frontispiece of the unfinished manuscript, came from Book II, in which the fallen angel Lucifer addresses his fellow devils, calling them

> *Thrones and Imperial Powers, off-spring of heaven,*
> *Ethereal Vertues;*

and asking them

> *. . . these Titles now*
> *Must we renounce, or changing still be called*
> *Princes of Hell?*

Lucifer suggests that since heaven is denied them, the devils should raise Cain on earth. That certainly sounds like a recipe for a cozy tale of malice domestic, but nearly sixty years later, not only the plot but the publishing fate of *Thrones, Dominations* are still open to speculation.

The very existence of the manuscript was not made public until 1976, when it was purchased by the Wade Center at Wheaton College in Illinois. There it can be read but not photocopied. Although the manuscript is owned by the center, the right to publish *Thrones, Dominations* rests with the Sayers estate.

By 1985, when I had completed the introduction and notes for an edition of Sayers's comedies *Busman's Honeymoon* and *Love All* and read a paper at the Modern Language Association, "Fossils in Cloud-Cuckoo Land, Real and Imagined Time in the Wimsey-Vane Chronicle," I convinced Sayers's son, Anthony Fleming, to consider publishing *Thrones, Dominations.*

The idea was to publish it "as is" and make the volume book length by adding other parts of the Wimsey saga such as "The Wimsey Papers," published in *The Spectator* from 1939 to 1940, and the spoof documents written in 1936 and 1937 by Sayers and her friends in what Sayers referred to as the "Wimsey Industry." Helen Simpson, who was responsible for overseeing such Detection Club projects as publishing *The Anatomy of Murder,* also arranged for the *Papers Relating to the Family of Wimsey* to be printed privately for their friends for Christmas 1936, as Sayers did with *An Account of Lord Mortimer Wimsey, the Hermit of the Wash* at Christmas 1937. Selections from these works and letters between Sayers and Wilfred Scott-Giles later appeared in 1977 in Scott-Giles's *The Wimsey Family;* so far as Scott-Giles knew, the Wimsey written record ended with the short story "Talboys," written in 1942 but not published until after Sayers's death.

When Anthony Fleming suddenly died in December 1985, he left the whole matter of publication to his heirs. Since then the Wade Center has purchased Sayers's letters from his estate, but there is still no agreement about any publication. At one time there were rumors that P. D. James, a longtime Sayers fan, might finish the book. She has not done so, and I still hope *Thrones, Dominations* will be published unfinished rather than turned into a Jamesian "variation" on a theme by Sayers or a Detection Club collaboration like *The Floating Admiral.* Apart from providing the pleasure of what Carolyn Heilbrun calls Sayers's civilized combination of "Conversation, Sweet Reason—and Gore," *Thrones, Dominations* represents a missing link in Sayers's creative development, both in the theater world and in its relationship to the real world of public events. But sometime in 1936 Sayers tossed its 170 pages into a packing box, which sat moldering in her attic at Witham until her death in 1957.

Her letters written to Simpson during July and August 1936 show Sayers was working on *Thrones* at the same time she was doing the novelization of *Busman's Honeymoon.* As a result, the answer may lie in the Simpson papers, if they still exist. Helen Simpson, another Oxford graduate and a successful author of mysteries, a biography, and a prize-winning novel, who had a delightful ability to tease Sayers and equal enthusiasm for detective fiction and quoting poetry, was perfectly cast as Sayers's chief confidante. As a writer for whom the give-and-take of ideas was an essential part of creation, Sayers always involved her friends in her work, using them as sounding boards, editors, and resource persons.

What is not clear in the letters is whether Simpson was also sent character sketches like those Sayers did for *Busman's Honeymoon*, reprinted in *Love All*, or if she read part of the manuscript itself. It appears Simpson had read a summary or, possibly, talked at length with Sayers about the novel on their frequent meetings in town.

As a full-time free-lancer, Sayers typically proceeded to the next book immediately, but she also worked on several projects at once. She did this with *Murder Must Advertise* and *The Nine Tailors*, as well as *Gaudy Night* and the play *Busman's Honeymoon*. In these later detective stories Sayers also made more use of real events and set them in the very recent past. For example, in *Gaudy Night* she refers to the Silver Jubilee of George V, which had taken place on May 6, 1935, just as she was finishing the novel, which was published that November.

A month later, in June 1935, Sayers completed the play *Busman's Honeymoon*. She then went to work on the novelization of the play, but it was not published until 1937 after the play had finally opened in December 1936. During the spring and summer of 1936 her friends took turns reading the novelization, and when she sent it back, Simpson wrote Sayers that she liked the "lushness" of its love scenes because everybody was tired of Noël Coward's work, where the "zenith of emotional expression was to offer the loved one a match for her cigarette."

By July 1936 Sayers was not only at work on *Thrones, Dominations* and rushing back and forth to London to help cast *Busman's Honeymoon*, which finally had a producer, but finishing her contributions to the Detection Club's *Anatomy of Murder* as well as *Papers Relating to the Family of Wimsey*. Simpson was overseeing both for publication. By October 1936 *Busman* had gone into rehearsal, and Sayers had become even more caught up in the world of the theater. She had also been asked to write the 1937 Canterbury Cathedral festival play and had accepted.

In February 1937 after reading the proofs, Simpson wrote to thank Sayers for her share of the *Busman* dedication, which gave "a very pretty name for . . . sticking my oar in." By March 1937 Sayers and her Wimsey Industry team—Muriel St. Clare Byrne, Wilfred Scott-Giles, and Helen Simpson—had gone to Cambridge University to put on a Wimsey program at Sidney Sussex College. By November 1937 Sayers wrote in her essay "Gaudy Night" that she saw "no end to the Wimseys this side the grave."

Since she went on to write *The Wimsey Papers* in 1939, as well as several short stories about Peter and Harriet's children, and comments to her friends showed the Wimsey saga was still evolving in her own imagination, why did she abandon *Thrones, Dominations*, especially since she already had worked out the story line and had told Simpson the scheme was so satisfactory "it hardly seems worthwhile writing the book"? Why, too, when wartime closed the theaters, didn't she return to it, the way T. S. Eliot returned to writing poetry?

The most popular explanations have been that since Sayers also wrote her first Canterbury Cathedral play, *The Zeal of Thy House*, in 1937, she must have decided to become a serious writer or got religion, turning away from mere fiction. But as Dr. Barbara Reynolds, who completed Sayers's Dante translation, has pointed out, Sayers was educated to be a scholar and had kept up her craft while she earned a living as a mystery writer, so that even her work on Dante was not the clear break with her past it has been taken to be. So far as fiction was concerned, Sayers had already abandoned a serious novel titled *Cat O'Mary* to write the play *Busman's Honeymoon* and *Gaudy Night*.

Dividing up Sayers's writing into separate categories does not seem to fit the facts. There is no doubt that Sayers fell in love with the theater as a result of the success of *Busman's Honeymoon* in 1936. Its comradely atmosphere became a logical extension of her writer's habit of working out her ideas in letters or conversations with friends, because for Sayers, "writing was a shared activity." But the play took over a year to find a backer, and it was not even being cast until early October 1936, several months after she wrote to Simpson about *Thrones*. That summer of 1936 Sayers had no way of knowing her play would be produced, much less achieve success.

As a result, neither the theory that a sudden passion for secular or religious theater, nor the fact that she was extremely busy lecturing and writing articles, seems to explain why Sayers failed to complete her final Wimsey mystery novel. Other possible reasons for abandoning *Thrones, Dominations* are the fact that this novel was far more explicit about sex than Sayers's earlier work, perhaps making it too outspoken for the mystery market, and, more important, I suspect, the fact that in this unfinished manuscript Sayers for the first time changed her thematic emphasis from private relationships to public commentary. Going public with her deep-seated convictions about the state of the realm was a process that she continued in *The Wimsey Papers*, then in her other non-Wimsey wartime books.

So what happened in 1936? Reading *Thrones, Dominations*, one sees clearly that the reader was to be shown—graphically—the significance of marriage as an institution, both for its participants and society at large. That was a logical theme for the newly married Wimseys, but unfortunately, given the time frame within which the story takes place—January to March 1936—Sayers's novel would also have been linked in the public's mind with the major event of 1936. This was the accession in January and the abdication that December of King Edward VIII (aka Prince Charming) to marry "the woman I love."

As the main theme of *Thrones, Dominations*, matrimony was to be developed dramatically by contrasting the fruitful relationship between newlyweds Harriet and Peter Wimsey with the barren, jealousy-ridden marriage of another rich young couple, Laurence and Rosamund Harwell. In addition, the Wimsey heir, Lord Peter's nephew Lord St. George, has once again gotten into a scrape over a woman and gone to his uncle Peter for support. But in this fragment, Jerry is shown as both impudent and unattractive, and, instead of quarreling over him, Lord Peter and his brother, the Duke of Denver, agree that Jerry's fitness to be head of the family is open to question. While Lord Peter is not quite ready to promise that Harriet will produce heirs to the duchy, the duke is anxious that she do so, and since Bredon Wimsey was born in the fall of 1936 (in the short story "The Haunted Policeman"), it is clear that Sayers meant Harriet to become pregnant by the end of February 1936. Quite possibly the announcement of her pregnancy was to be the ending of *Thrones*.

Sayers may have felt that she was imitating life too closely by paralleling a public event too recent to be forgotten by her readers. Unlike many intellectuals, Sayers did not think that Edward VIII was the victim of the Establishment's "Old Gang." She thought—as do most historians today—that Edward VIII was a lightweight whose loss was good riddance because he had not "played the game."

But, while the accession of Edward's younger brother, George VI, guaranteed the continuity of the royal line—and a future Elizabeth II—as Prince of Wales Edward VIII had been very popular with the Commonwealth. His abdication struck a heavy blow at the roots of the British empire, whose culture Sayers considered a vital part of Western civilization. The parallel with the Wimseys was clear: if Lord St. George did not inherit the duchy, it would go to Lord Peter and his sons, who could be trusted to do their duty.

Once a year had passed and George VI had been crowned, it would have been reasonable for Sayers to return to the novel. Although Sayers wrote some Wimsey short stories, and she and Simpson also exchanged news about other Wimsey activities, by 1938 intelligent observers saw war looming. Simpson had decided that the poets and scholars had wrongly allowed themselves to be driven from political life, only too happy to criticize and not to lead. Suiting her actions to her words, Simpson ran as a Liberal Party candidate for Parliament on the Isle of Wight, with a platform about adequate housing and medical facilities, and most of all, the concern that universal education had been divorced from humane letters, making people more exploitable than before. This was an idea echoed by Sayers's own dissatisfaction with advertising.

Helen Simpson's wit and intelligence, as well as her serious convictions, had made a lasting impression on Sayers when in February 1940 their friendship was cruelly ended. Simpson had major surgery, which first led to her enforced departure from London's heavy bombing, then to her death that October. It is a testament to the strength of their friendship that the very busy matron of the hospital took time to write a condolence note to Sayers, telling her how much Simpson had cared for her and adding that she knew how sad Sayers would find life without her.

It does not take a great stretch of the imagination to wonder if Sayers might have found going back to work on *Thrones, Dominations* too full of memories of Simpson. From Sayers's moving tribute to Simpson published in *The Spectator* in January 1941, it is also clear that Sayers now took as her own the concerns and goals Simpson held for society. Her description of Simpson's agenda for the future reads like a summary of Sayers's wartime books like *Begin Here* and *The Mind of the Maker*. In "The Mysterious English" Sayers also echoed Australian-born Simpson's comment at the fall of France that "it's bad, but I think it will be all right . . . because the English are rather a wonderful people." Is the unfinished state of *Thrones, Dominations* a tribute to their friendship?

Whatever the answer, *Thrones, Dominations* is still vintage Sayers. For Sayers, like P. D. James, a story's setting gives the reader the "particularity" that makes it "real." Since she had become fascinated with the theater, it is not surprising that Sayers set this story in the London world of the arts. Besides Harriet Wimsey, half a dozen major and minor characters are artists, writers, publishers, or actors, playwrights, and producers of West End plays. Its dramatic but talky scenes are very like those in her witty, wordy theater play *Love All*, written about 1938. The close relation of *Love All* to *Thrones* in theme and setting may mean that she abandoned the novel to do the play.

But the sequence of events in the manuscript is also a mystery, because its pages were numbered at the Wade Center the way they came out of the packing box. In her usual fashion Sayers did number the pages of specific scenes, which have been kept together, but their order is open to question. Each reader has to decide whether to take the story as it came from the box or to rearrange it.

Since Sayers customarily wrote a story in chronological order, I chose to arrange the scenes logically from the three key events mentioned in the manuscript. They are the (fictional) execution of murderer Frank Crutchley on January 10, 1936, the first day of Oxford

University's Hilary (or Winter) Term on January 19, 1936, and the death of King George V on January 20, 1936.

The last event in the novel *Busman's Honeymoon* was Frank Crutchley's execution night. In *Thrones, Dominations* that same event determines the date of the dinner party reluctantly given for the newly married Wimseys by their sister-in-law the duchess of Denver. In a discussion between the duke and the duchess, it is agreed that their son and heir, Lord St. George (Jerry), must be present. Since he is still a student at Oxford, their party has to take place before January 19, 1936, when his winter term begins. Accordingly, the very amusing dinner party is held on January 17, just after the Peter Wimseys return from France.

In my reorganization, the story opens in Paris, where Harriet and Peter have fled after Crutchley's execution on January 10. In scene 1 on January 11, Peter's uncle, Paul Delagardie, and his French friend, M. Daumier, are dining at the best hotel in Paris and discussing English marriage customs. They relate their theories to two couples in the dining room, who turn out to be Lawrence and Rosamund Harwell and the Peter Wimseys. Paul Delagardie knows both couples, so he takes great delight in telling M. Daumier his theories are wrong. Gorgeous as she is, Rosamund is a wife, not a mistress, and Peter did not marry Harriet for her money. Instead, both were love matches. Harwell, who is wealthy and enjoys backing theatrical productions, had rescued Rosamund from work as a model when her father was imprisoned for embezzling theatrical funds, while his nephew, Wimsey, had rescued his wife from a murder charge.

The second scene is the duchess of Denver's formal dinner party on January 17, with which she hopes to launch her new sister-in-law into Polite Society. (The duchess feels convinced that this is a Herculean task but is equally convinced Harriet is avid for the opportunity.)

Sayers wrote two different versions of this set piece, with somewhat different guests present. They include Helen's boring sister and brother-in-law, a publisher and his statuesque wife (beauty in wives is a minor theme throughout), a gossip columnist who wanted to marry Lord Peter, and an elderly lady with her current protégé, a young French painter who is an interested, ironic observer of the English. The painter is doing a portrait of Rosamund Harwell, whose beauty is discussed at the party. After the ladies leave, he suddenly announces that he wants to paint Harriet, too.

The scene then moves to the Wimseys' new home at South Audley Square. While Lord Peter is gone on business, Harriet's writing is interrupted by the arrival of a coach and four. Peeking from the window she sees old Lady Severn and Thames, Peter's godmother, who has come to inspect both Harriet and the house. The old lady takes a fancy to Harriet (who stands up well to her impertinent questions) but insists on inspecting the staff and the house from top to bottom. When Lord Peter returns the old lady asks what they plan to name their children, and he replies, "Matthew, Mark, Luke and John, Keziah, Jemima, and Karen-Haputt. After that we shall begin on the nine muses and the Kings of Israel and Judea." There follows a short scene with Peter and Harriet alone, in which Sayers made much of the contrast between their elegant mansion filled with beautiful family things, and the Harwells' modern service flat with its sexy sea green boudoir and spoiled pug dog. (That flat seems to have been suggested by Simpson, who wrote Sayers that a "beastly service flat in Grosvenor House done up exactly like the most expensive prison . . . will suit them very well.")

The fifth scene takes place in the "expensive prison" on January 20. Lawrence Harwell sits up all night to hear the BBC bulletins about George V, coming to bed only when the king dies. He tells Rosamund he must close his theaters for the official mourning period, but she is less concerned about his business problems than about her social obligation to wear black. True moderns, they both find the end of an era thrilling.

In scene 6 on January 21, Sayers contrasts the Harwells' reactions to those of the Wimsey connections in a series of tiny vignettes. Harriet walks down Oxford Street, soberly taking the pulse of the city as it puts on official mourning. Peter visits his brother-in-law, Superintendent Charles Parker at Scotland Yard. Peter is melancholy at the end of an era, while Parker is more concerned with security arrangements for all the foreign royals coming for the funeral. On the French Riviera, Paul Delagardie, after receiving the formal condolences of M. Daumier, suddenly decides to come home.

By contrast, Rosamund Harwell lunches with a young admirer, playwright-novelist Claude Amory. When Rosamund brings Amory back to her apartment, she finds her ex-con father has arrived in London. Then Peter returns home to Harriet, seeking tea and sympathy.

On January 23 the body of George V was brought by train from Sandringham and taken in solemn procession down Whitehall to lie in state at Westminster Hall until his funeral on January 28. In scene 7 the Wimseys watch the funeral procession from a Whitehall balcony with the young French painter, who says to Lord Peter, standing there motionless with his hands clenched on the railing:

> "You are a remarkable nation . . . you permit a casual crowd to arrange itself with . . . a few unarmed policemen. Then you take your new king and all the male heirs to the throne, throw in the crown of England for good measure . . . and walk them slowly for two miles through the open streets of the capital. . . ."
>
> "This is just a village funeral," said Peter. "Nobody would dream of making a disturbance."
>
> The young painter replied, "You think of yourselves as a practical people, yet your empire is held together by nothing but a name and a dream. You laugh at your own traditions and are confident the world will respect them. And it does. . . ."
>
> "It may not last," said Peter Wimsey.

After the funeral procession the Wimseys meet the Harwells and take them back to South Audley Square, where Rosamund and Harriet thoroughly misunderstand one another and Rosamund takes a violent dislike to Peter, who she decides patronizes Harriet. Harriet later compounds their misunderstanding by mentioning a new play by Claude Amory, Rosamund's admirer, to a well-known producer. Annoyed at Harriet's interference, Rosamund seduces her husband into backing Amory's play against his better judgment.

The last two scenes (which are numbered first, thanks to the luck of the draw at the Wade Center) occur soon after Paul Delagardie returns to London. Peter and Harriet talk very frankly about their sexual relationship, with Harriet asking Peter outright why he didn't use "caveman" tactics on her. Peter tells her to ask his uncle Paul. When Paul Delagardie comes to tea, Harriet does so, and is told the story of how Delagardie introduced his young nephew to the joys and responsibilities of sex with the aid of a French mistress.

And that's the end of the manuscript. Anyone reading *Thrones, Dominations* feels sure that murder will out but can only speculate on exactly who, where, when, and why. If Dr. Barbara Reynolds locates Helen Simpson's papers, they may provide further clues, but it may still remain a genuine mystery how the story was to conclude or why Sayers left it unfinished. In any case, I hope yet to see it published.

It Was the Cat!

CATHERINE AIRD

It may seem a little inappropriate to use a quotation from Gilbert and Sullivan's light opera *H.M.S. Pinafore* when writing about the short stories of DLS, but members of the genus *Felix* species *domesticus* do figure more than somewhat in this particular aspect of her exceptionally wide-reaching oeuvre, reminding us of DLS's fondness for their independent ways.

For various reasons her short stories do not seem to have had the same attention that the rest of her many writings—the full-length detective stories, the theological plays, her work on Dante, and so forth—have attracted: indeed some commentators have been less than enthusiastic about them.

Can they have been cast aside on the grounds of size rather than skill? I think that would be a pity, because if any one aspect of DLS's character is clearly outstanding, it is her sheer competence. Obviously she must have been a firm believer in the aphorism "if something is worth doing at all, it is worth doing well." Nothing could exemplify this better than her workmanlike approach to the art and craft of the detective short story, not only as a practitioner but as a distinguished editor of the literary form as well.

Her introductory essays to the various volumes of Gollancz's series titled *Great Short Stories of Detection, Mystery and Horror*, which she also edited, are masterly in their grasp of the history and form of this aspect of detection writing. They remain an object lesson for those who would follow the same path as reader or writer, although some now may want to challenge her assertion (made in 1928) that the really brilliant woman detective has yet to be created.

These essays, authoritative and challenging as they are, demonstrate the breadth of her intellect as well as a range of knowledge of her subject, making them still readable and relevant over sixty years later, though I find myself still undecided about her statement that there might only be as few as six deceptions available to the mystery monger.

We should remember that a short story is not a little story, nor is it a full-length novel either shrunk or compressed. There is a nice (in the precise sense of that much-abused word) distinction between the size of an idea that will provide substance for a short story and the larger conception that will furnish a full-length book, and DLS made no errors here.

We have all read long detective novels in which the plot hangs on too slender a thread, sufficient really only for the smaller canvas of a short story. Oddly enough the converse does not seem to apply: seldom indeed do we read short stories at whose end the reader is entitled to feel that that same thread could have borne the weight of a full-length novel.

In my view the best comparison comes from the world of art—between, say, an Elizabethan miniature painting by Nicholas Hilliard and a wall-size canvas of the proportions and composition of a Winterhalter or Benjamin West. If anything, the former form requires the greater skill. The bigger the canvas, the more room there is for error (and perhaps error retrieval as well). I am not sure if a similar parallel can be drawn with musical composition—between, say, a divertissement and a symphony.

This is not to imply that either form does not require the author's full attention. Quite the reverse, in fact. It is abundantly clear that when DLS put her hand to that particular plow she gave it—the short story—her full attention.

In the normal course of a detective-novelist's thought processes during a normal working day, usable (and reusable and unusable!)

ideas surface that are perforce supernumerary to the particular work at hand. Indeed, it would be strange if this did not happen. The economical writer (which we know DLS to have been) keeps some of these for her next book and some for future short stories to be written "upon the mellowing of occasion." These latter sheddings (I cannot bring myself to call them bite-sized pieces, but this is what they are) go into the wise worker's notebook as a squirrel's acorns go into a hoard for winter.

It is interesting to record that DLS's economy extended to using again in her full-length books names of characters and places that had made their debut in the short stories—Miss Gladys Twitterton, Crichton's and Wilbraham—and were just too good not to reappear. More than that, the writing of some of the short stories themselves must have stimulated the author to develop an idea, a background, a theme into a new book. There are clear precursory signs of *The Five Red Herrings* in "The Stolen Stomach," the seaside (and an advertising agency) in "The Man with No Face," and an East Anglian village seen from the standpoint of the squire rather than the church in "The Bone of Contention." *Gaudy Night* could not have had a better dummy-run than "Murder at Pentecost."

There is yet another aspect of DLS's short stories (and, indeed, to her full-length novels, too) that was brought about by her study of her great predecessors in the genre. By-products of those studies are especially evident in her earlier stories, such as the way in which "The Cave of Ali Baba" resembles the situation in Conan Doyle's "The Final Problem" and "The Empty House." "The Dragon's Head" is a treasure-hunt tale reminiscent of Doyle's "The Musgrave Ritual" or even Poe's "The Gold Bug," with a flavor of its own because of Lord Peter's interest in old books. The tantalizing Doyle mannerism of referring to unpublished cases can be found in the first paragraph of "The Article in Question."

"The Footsteps That Ran" is clearly influenced by G. K. Chesterton's Father Brown story "The Queer Feet." There are overtones, too, of Baroness Orczy's "Old Man in the Corner" method of detection in "The Man with No Face," and of R. Austin Freeman in "The Man with Copper Fingers" and "The Image in the Mirror."

Due tribute by DLS to these literary progenitors may usually be found in a reference to the author, but it is this very duality of both harking back and being more than up-to-the-minute that makes her work so perennially fascinating and allows her to take her place with her "great contemporaries."

As far as is known the very first of her short stories to achieve publication was "Who Calls the Tune," which appeared in *Blue Moon*, published by the Mutual Admiration Society in 1917 and now virtually unobtainable. It is an imaginary tale of a dead millionaire called to render his account of his life, not, as is customary, to Saint Peter, but to the Devil for the purpose of establishing how many years his soul must spend in purgatory. It is interesting to record that twenty-two years later her play *The Devil to Pay* was produced at Canterbury Cathedral, although it may be stretching a point to argue that this interest in purgatory also foreshadowed her interest in Dante and his circles of hell.

The majority of DLS's short stories have been published in three volumes of collected stories. These are *Lord Peter Views the Body*, composed entirely of Lord Peter Wimsey stories; *Hangman's Holiday*, made up of four Lord Peter stories, six that feature Montague Egg, and two others; and *In the Teeth of the Evidence and Other Stories*. Two more Lord Peter stories, five Montague Egg ones, and ten called simply "Other Stories" make up this last collection.

Two stories that had first appeared in *Detection Medley*, edited by John Rhode, were later included in a paperback called *Striding Folly* in 1972. The third short story in this book was "Talboys," which had been written in 1942 but was not published until this time.

The short stories therefore fall into three groups—the Lord Peter stories, the Montague Egg tales, and those with neither character as hero/detective. Only one is really about the supernatural, and that is "The Cyprian Cat," which is, unusually for DLS, written in the first-person singular and concerns a man afraid of, and physically sensitive to, cats. (The word *allergy* was not in common usage at the time it was written.) We are very gradually meant to believe the "victim" (by her persistent refusal to cross running water) is a witch who has taken the form of a Cyprian cat.

But DLS seems to have eschewed writing further tales involving the supernatural. The only other of her short stories that could be said to contain anything really inexplicable is "The Leopard Lady," who manifests herself in the person of Miss Smith, the girl with the yellow eyes like cat's eyes, "who should have been called Melusine." Here the reader is rather flatteringly assumed to know the ancient French legend of Melusine, a water fairy of great power and wealth, married to Raymond, son of a *Comte de la Foret*, who found her near a spring in the forest of Colombiers in Poitou. She is connected in old folklore with both the Banshee and the Mermaid. Needless to say, however, the murder in this story is both perfectly plausible and quite up-to-date.

Similarly, the point-device (if I may be forgiven the pun) of "The Article in Question" is given to the reader in French. It is well established that DLS expected and exacted a high standard of literacy from her readers (or the energy to resort to a dictionary or similar works of reference). I think this is one of the ways in which she somehow contrived to enter into a subtle collaboration with her readers, the ultimate outcome of which was that they are made to feel that they share her erudition.

This is a gift, a precious gift. There are, perhaps, readers who have even been led to study the comic satires of Petronius, that licentious author of the least noble Latin slang of them all, as a result of the titillating reference to him in "The Unprincipled Affair of the Practical Joker." Others possibly have read something about the author into Wimsey's wry observation in the same story that it is sheer foolishness for women to have a sense of honor in affairs of the heart.

The amateur psychologist in us all cannot fail to have noticed that at least two stories have, very unusually, as their motive for murder a quite genuine indebtedness to their victims on the part of the murderers. Perhaps, like Harriet Vane, the author did not like the idea of being beholden to anyone. Similarly, there are at least two stories in which a jealous husband has wrongly inferred infidelity on the part of his wife and the intended victim. And if any suspect has a cheerful, debonair, devil-may-care manner, you can be pretty sure he didn't do it.

"Talboys" comes long after all the other short stories have seen the light of day. It, as every reader knows, concerns Lord Peter as a married man—nay, a much-married happy man—with three sons. Since it was not published when it was written in 1942, it is not unreasonable to suppose that this was by wish of the author. It may be—as detective short stories go—somewhat too thin for the canon, but as a reflection of how DLS would have liked life to have been it is both painfully revealing and sad. No one relishes having their dreams exposed and trodden on. Look on it kindly.

The Lord Peter stories start with the invaluable background of a ready-made main character and ambience—the equivalent of the flesh-colored "carnation" on which the detail of a miniature painting is created. This is not the case in the Montague Egg stories, and they are in some cases the less entertaining for it. There are, for instance, altogether fewer layers of meaning in the Montague Egg stories—and more plain deduction. One particularly gets the feeling the Egg stories might be instances in which the stone that was set at nought by the author for a full-length book has become the cornerstone of a short story. And while one appreciates that their author has caught the professional jauntiness associated by the average reader with the occupation of commercial traveler, ironically Montague Egg is not as convincing a character as Lord Peter Wimsey. On more than one occasion Egg is described by the author as young, yet youth is not the impression made on my mind by either his speech or behavior. In some ways he is almost a "marked-down" Bunter without Bunter's omniscience. Yet the kernel of the story is, as always, perfectly sound.

In spite of the fact that the payoff line is usually a rhyming homiletic from "The Salesman's Handbook," most of the stories featuring Montague Egg depend on observation or timing and amply demonstrate "that quiet enjoyable of the logical" about which E. M. Wrong wrote in his memorable introduction to *Tales of Crime and Detection*.

Incidentally, Wrong's theory that detective fiction did not flourish until the public had an idea of what constitutes proof was neatly taken further by DLS in her marvelous comments on detective fiction. She suggested that the detective story proper (as opposed to the crime story) could not begin to flourish until public sympathy had veered around to the side of law and order. Montague Egg was a man very much on the side of law and order, although never forgetting his duty to his employers, Messrs. Plummett and Rose, Wine Merchants. These stories are admittedly slighter than those in which Lord Peter figures, but like all of DLS's work of this period they contain sad echoes of the great financial crashes and scandals of her day. Absconding financiers cast shadows over the lives of ordinary people then as now. They would have been real enough to the customers of Montague Egg, traveling representative *extraordinaire*.

Some of the stories show a topicality that is not easy to evaluate at this distance in time—for instance, Landsteiner's method of blood grouping, the crux of "Blood Sacrifice," was later overtaken by a different notation altogether when blood groups became the more familiar A, B, or O.

DLS was truly prescient in the use of voice printing. It is common knowledge among police and the criminal fraternity today but was as impractical and futuristic in 1928, the date of "The Adventurous Exploit of the Cave of Ali Baba," as her Court-Windlesham helicopter.

Some stories show a great and joyous inventiveness, in particular "The Inspiration of Mr. Budd" and "The Piscatorial Farce of the Stolen Stomach," although here the title was unusually revealing—perhaps in deference to the greater sensibilities to human anatomy of an earlier generation.

Some demand greater mental exercise on the part of the reader—"The Queen's Square" and "The Fascinating Problem of Uncle Meleager's Will" are two of them—while the trompe l'oeil of "The Haunted Policeman" was clearly an idea waiting to be used, and use it DLS did. And some, notably "Suspicion," have their sting—like a scorpion's—in their tail. All the short stories share both the veri-similitude and the meticulous attention to detail that we, her readers, have come to expect in all her work. The short stories then may be read in the secure knowledge that—to quote an even greater East Anglian Christian woman writer of another and much earlier age—"All will be well."

With acknowledgments to a long and lively correspondence with Philip L. Scowcroft.

Where the Bodies
Are Buried

The Real Murder Cases in the Crime Novels
of Dorothy L. Sayers

SHARYN MCCRUMB

There is ample evidence in the writings of Dorothy L. Sayers to demonstrate that she knew about true crime cases in Britain and France, both as current events and as historical occurrences. Her works are sprinkled with references to actual crimes, all carefully chosen to reflect the fictional crime at hand. However, with one exception there is little to indicate that she was influenced by any actual case when it came to the creation of the plots of her own works of crime fiction. In this, she differs markedly from her fellow mystery writer Agatha Christie, with whom she is often linked by those who consider them the grande dames of the "cozy" mystery. In fact, the two have little in common in terms of plotting or literary philosophy.

Agatha Christie often used real incidents, changed and sensationalized, as the basis for her crime novels, although she always added her own inimitable twists to spice up real life. For example, in Christie's *Murder on the Orient Express*, one can see the personalities in the Lindbergh kidnapping case magically transported to a European luxury train; and thirties socialite and murderess Elvira Barney appears as a murder suspect named Bess in *At Bertram's Hotel*;

but in the novel the murderer is Bess's daughter, whose name is—Elvira. Perhaps when one writes more than eighty mystery novels, personal inspiration for mayhem wears thin.

Dorothy L. Sayers, less prolific with only a dozen crime novels and three collections of mystery short stories, may have shared Christie's penchant for inventing puzzles for the reader, but she was less inclined to ground her tales in the reality of true crime. Sayers seemed to delight in thinking up ingenious if impractical modes of murder to test the readers' wits. Such flights of fancy seldom reflect the realities of true crime. Reality seemed too tame to intrigue Dorothy L. Sayers: she preferred an intellectual kingdom of ciphers, timetables, and bizarre coincidences.

The first novel featuring Lord Peter Wimsey appeared in 1923. The plot for *Whose Body?*—the finding of a corpse in a bathtub—seems to have been inspired by a parlor game played at Oxford during Sayers's years as a student at Somerville College. It is the contrived puzzle of the murderous medical examiner that intrigued the author, and she devised it herself.

Have His Carcase, published in 1932, is a puzzle mystery that has not worn well, because its plot turns on a medical condition that was not well known at the time Sayers wrote the novel; now that the characteristics of hemophilia are common knowledge, the reader spots the gimmick as soon as the body is discovered. The crime is the sort of intellectual puzzle that novelists delight in but real life never seems to produce. A man is found murdered on a rock in a bay, with the tide coming in. His throat has been cut, and the blood has not yet clotted, suggesting that the murder has just occurred. Several hundred pages later, the sleuths deduce what is apparent to all modern readers considerably earlier: the victim was a hemophiliac. In *Such a Strange Lady*, Janet Hitchman attributes the inspiration for *Have His Carcase* to Sayers's great friend John Cournos, a Russian-born writer with considerable experience in codes. It is interesting to note, however, that the novel was written in 1931, the year that Spain's King Alphonso XIII and Queen Eugenie were deposed and exiled from Spain, after which their marriage foundered—because King Alphonso never forgave his queen for transmitting hemophilia to two of their sons. (Like the Russian Czarina Alexandra, Queen Victoria Eugenie of Spain was descended from England's Queen Victoria, the most famous carrier of the hereditary disease.) Certainly the Spanish incident would have served as a topical reminder of the fictional possibilities of hemophilia.

In Sayers's novels *Murder Must Advertise* and *The Five Red Herrings*, it is not the crime but the ambience that is based on real life. The former, in which Lord Peter takes a job as an advertising copywriter at Pym's, echoes Dorothy L. Sayers's experience at Bensons. *The Five Red Herrings* is a plot devised to fit a setting: the town of Kirkcudbright, where for several years Sayers and her husband spent their summer holidays. *Gaudy Night,* a reunion at an Oxford college closely resembling Sayers's alma mater Somerville, also seems inspired more by setting and philosophy than by any desire to practice the mechanics of detection.

In *The Remarkable Case of Dorothy L. Sayers,* Catherine Kenney suggests that *The Unpleasantness at the Bellona Club* may have been inspired by an old joke: that in English clubs one cannot tell the live members from the dead ones. There is no evidence that such an incident ever occurred. In *Clouds of Witness*, Sayers indulged her love of esoteric knowledge by examining the procedure for the trial of a peer.

The Nine Tailors was inspired by the author's childhood in the fen country, and by a book that Sayers found in a secondhand bookshop: *Change Ringing*, by C. A. W. Troyte. The unlikely method of murder was devised to fit a narrative in which Sayers was more interested in change ringing and philosophy than in detection. *Unnatural Death* features another unlikely method of murder: killing one's victim by injecting air into his vein with a hypodermic needle. Critics and medical experts alike have called this a decidedly tricky method of murder, more likely to fail than not. One would need luck and a *large* syringe.

The one Sayers novel that could have been suggested by an actual case is *Strong Poison*, published in 1930 by Gollancz. The plight of Harriet Vane in this novel, the fifth in the Wimsey series, is reminiscent of the case of Florence Maybrick. Both the fictional heroine and the real Liverpool matron were charged with murder after the death by arsenic poisoning of their mates. Maybrick, an Alabama belle who married an English cotton broker twenty-three years her senior, found herself saddled with a hypochrondriac who was unfaithful to her and who boasted of taking arsenic as an aphrodisiac. In 1887 after six years of marriage, Florence learned that her husband had a mistress; she also discovered that he was in severe financial difficulties. Florence consoled herself with Alfred Brierly, a friend of James Maybrick. In March 1889 Florence and Brierly spent a weekend together in London; her husband found out about his escapade and beat her. A few weeks afterward, Florence went to the local chemist and bought a dozen arsenic-based flypapers. Five days later she purchased two dozen more from a different shop. Matters between the Maybricks were deteriorating quickly: James made a new will, excluding his wife from any inheritance. On April 28, 1889, Maybrick became ill. Florence told the doctor that her husband had been taking a "white powder." Two weeks later Maybrick died, and his enraged relatives searched Battlecrease House for evidence against Florence. In her room they found a packet labeled "Arsenic Poison For Cats." An autopsy revealed traces of arsenic in the body, and Florence was tried for his murder. Despite the fact that Maybrick took arsenic himself as an aphrodisiac, Florence was convicted of his murder, though the verdict might have said more about the jury's opinion of her adultery than it did about her guilt in the matter of her husband's death. She received the death penalty, but the sentence was commuted to life imprisonment. Despite appeals for her release from Presidents Grover Cleveland and William McKinley, and from Florence's own attorney, Charles Russell, who became Lord Chief Justice of England, she served fifteen years for a crime that she probably did not commit, emerging from prison in 1904 at the age of forty-one. She reassumed her maiden name, Florence Chandler, and returned to the United States, where she died in poverty in 1941—fifty-two years after the death of her husband.

In Sayers's plot, which uses some of the facets of the Maybrick story, mystery writer Harriet Vane becomes angry with her lover, Philip Boyes, because after declaring that he did not believe in marriage, he has decided after two years of cohabiting that he will make an honest woman of her. Harriet feels that she has been betrayed and made a fool of by this romantic probation. Shortly thereafter, Harriet buys arsenic from a chemist shop as part of the research for her mystery novel. When Philip Boyes dies of arsenic poisoning, Harriet Vane is charged with murder. The other suspect, Boyes's uncle, is seemingly eliminated because he shared Boyes's last meal—an omelette—but did not become ill himself, thus apparently eliminating that meal as the source of the poison. Wimsey discovers that the uncle is an arsenic-eater; the poisoned omelette did not affect him because he had developed a tolerance for arsenic. This is not an exact rendering of the Maybrick case: the innocent woman, her lover, and the wicked arsenic-eater are all present, but their roles have been skewed to suit the author.

Despite the fact that Sayers's plots were contrived from art rather than life, there is ample evidence that the author was well versed in the details of famous crime cases. She was familiar with contemporary causes célèbres, and with infamous cases throughout history. Her knowledge of crime ranged from a discussion of Sawney Bean, the Scottish cannibal from medieval times, in Sayers's *Omnibus of Crime*, to her 1937 essay "The Murder of Julia Wallace," an analysis of the Liverpool murder case, speculating on whether the convicted man did in fact murder his wife. On January 20, 1931, William Herbert Wallace, a Liverpool insurance agent, was summoned by telephone to a meeting with a potential client at an address that proved to be fictitious. He claimed that when he returned home from this wild-goose chase, he found his wife, Julia, dead in the parlor, battered to death by a poker. Wallace's bloodstained mackintosh was lying beneath the body. The police did not believe his story about the mysterious telephone summons and charged him with the murder on February 2. At Wallace's trial the judge summed up the evidence in the defendant's favor, but the jury nonetheless brought in a verdict of guilty and sentenced him to death. The case was overturned on appeal and Wallace was freed, to suffer suspicion and ill health until his death from a kidney disorder in 1933. In January 1981 broadcast journalist Roger Wilkes decided to reopen the file on the Wallace case for a radio documentary. His broadcast appeal for information uncovered new evidence identifying the murderer of Julia Wallace—and proving the innocence of William Herbert Wallace.

Besides these extended studies of nonfictitious crimes, Sayers made frequent references to well-known cases in her fiction, sprinkling topical references throughout the early Wimsey novels to lend verisimilitude to the narrative. Each time she mentioned a true case within the course of a novel, the case always echoed a theme of the novel or a clue to the identity of the fictional murderer.

In *Whose Body?* Lord Peter attends a luncheon during the course of the investigation, and the conversation about the mysterious body in Thipps's bath leads to a remark by Mrs. Tommy Frayle about "the man who was hanged for murdering three brides in a bath." She is referring, of course, to the infamous George Joseph Smith, who married women for their money and then did away with them, changing his name but never his method of murder. Smith came to trial in 1915 after the father of one of his early victims read about the death of Margaret Elizabeth Lofty, Smith's third victim, in the bath at Highgate, London. He was—as Mrs. Frayle noted in *Whose Body?*—hanged for the murders (on August 13, 1915, at Maidstone Prison).

Later in the novel, George Joseph Smith is mentioned by name, along with Edmond de la Pommerais, as criminal heroes to the wicked physician Sir Julian Freke, villain of the piece. Dr. Edmond de la Pommerais, a French physician with considerable social ambition, married the wealthy Mlle Dubisy in 1861, becoming rich after the death of his mother-in-law, whom he attended in her last illness. When two years later this fortune was gone, he arranged to insure his mistress's life for half a million francs, whereupon she died of cholera while under his care. The insurance company exhumed the two bodies, and de la Pommerais was charged with poisoning his victims with digitalis. He was guillotined for the murder of his mistress in 1864.

Both these crimes are appropriate to the plot of *Whose Body?*: the novel's central mystery, a body in the bath, naturally suggests George Joseph Smith, who killed women in the bath, and the poisoning physician de la Pommerais foreshadows the revelation of the villain of the novel: the murderer is a medical doctor.

In *Strong Poison* when Wimsey is discussing the trial of Harriet Vane with his mother, the dowager duchess of Denver, they note that some murders are committed because the killers enjoy the sensation of killing. The duchess mentions Landru, referring to the French Bluebeard Henri Desire Landru, a lethal lothario who seduced 283 women and persuaded them to hand over their money and property to him for investment. Ten of these women he murdered. Landru's method for attracting victims was to place notices in newspapers, advertising himself as a widower with two children and a comfortable income, seeking a suitable widow with a view to matrimony. When women answered the ad, he would seduce them with promises of marriage and make off with their money. Landru was caught when one of the swindled women discovered him romancing one of her successors. Police discovered that Landru kept a meticulous notebook detailing the expenses incurred in his amorous ventures, and the stove in his house was found to contain 295 bone fragments from his victims. He was guillotined in Paris on February 25, 1922. Sayers's familiarity with the Landru case reflects a knowledge of current events rather than an interest in criminology; she was working near Paris as a secretary to her Oxford friend Eric Whelpton during the time that the Landru trial was a cause célèbre.

Clouds of Witness concerns the murder trial of Lord Peter's brother, the duke of Denver, in the House of Lords. The logical case for the author to mention to lend verisimilitude to the novel is the trial of Lawrence, Lord Ferrers, and she does. In chapter 2 Inspector Parker and Lord Peter are discussing the seriousness of Gerald's plight, and Wimsey wonders whether peers can be hanged if convicted of murder. Parker replies, "They certainly hanged Earl Ferrers in 1760." Ferrers, the last nobleman to be executed in England, had a history of violence that included beating and stabbing his servants and battering his wife, who endured his abuse for six years before leaving him. In 1760 Lord Ferrers became convinced that his elderly steward, John Johnson, was plotting against him. He demanded to see the household accounts, insisted that Johnson had falsified them, and then shot the steward as he knelt begging for his life. Johnson died of his wounds a few hours later, and the attending physician had Ferrers arrested for murder. He was tried in the House of Lords, found guilty, and hanged at Tyburn on May 5, 1760.

The other case mentioned in *Clouds of Witness* is simply referred to by the city in which it happened. In chapter 3 Wimsey and the police superintendent at Ripley are discussing the need to trace a motorcycle that was seen in the vicinity on the night of Denis Cathcart's death. The superintendent remarks: "It's not altogether easy to trace a motor-cycle without knowing the number. Look at the Bournemouth murder." When the novel was published in 1927, English readers would have recognized this reference as readily as Americans today would know to whom "the Milwaukee murders" referred. Today, though, the crime is all but forgotten, and other Bournemouth murders, most notably the Rattenbury-Stoner case, come to mind at the mention of the city, but these cases occurred later than the publication of *Clouds of Witness*. The superintendent's "Bournemouth murder" was the slaying on December 22, 1921, of Irene Wilkins. She had placed an ad in the *Morning Post* asking for work as a school cook, and when a telegram came from Bournemouth asking her to come down by train to interview for a job, she did so at once. The next day her bludgeoned body was found in a field outside the city; she had not been raped or robbed. Almost the only clue to her assailant was a trail of tire tracks in the road near the body. The police identified the tires as Dunlop Magnums and began an area-wide search for all cars fitted with that brand of tire. The search turned up Allaway, and samples of his handwriting matched that on the telegram. Despite the apparent absence of motive in the case, Allaway was convicted and executed at Winchester in the summer of 1922.

It is interesting to note that most of these murders involved the same sort of case: that of a man taking financial advantage of a woman and then killing her. Sayers aptly chose these crimes to mention, because in both *Clouds of Witness* and *Strong Poison* the murdered man was romantically linked to a woman with money (heiress Lady Mary Wimsey and successful author Harriet Vane), while the men themselves were ne'er-do-wells. In her fictional cases Sayers turns the tables on the sponging ladykillers by seeing to it that it is the men who die, while the women are rescued from future unhappiness at their hands. Those familiar with Sayers's own life may reflect upon the connection (if any) to the fact that for many years Sayers herself was the breadwinner in her marriage to Mac Fleming.

Unnatural Death contains the most thorough discussion of true crime, a conversation in chapter 8 between Lord Peter and Charles Parker about the number of people who get away with murder. Wimsey points out that most murderers are caught because they try the trick once too often. It is only on the third or fourth go-round that they are caught. He mentions George Joseph Smith again, whose bathtub method got him caught on Wife Number Three.

Wimsey's second example of a killer who failed to practice moderation is Dr. William Palmer, a Staffordshire physician whose first hobby—extravagant and unsuccessful gambling—led to a second hobby: poisoning his relatives. He disposed of his mother-in-law in order to inherit her money. Four of his children died in infancy. As his gambling debts mounted, the doctor insured his wife and brother for large sums, and they conveniently died. Then his illegitimate children and his creditors perished. He might have got away with mass murder if he had not added John Parsons Cook to his list of victims. Cook's only offense was to accompany Palmer to the races, and to win while Palmer lost. At the supper party that evening Cook became ill, and under the care of his physician friend, he died. Cook's stepfather demanded an autopsy, and traces of antimony were found. Palmer was convicted of murder and hanged outside Stafford Gaol on June 14, 1856.

Wimsey also mentions the case of Welsh solicitor Herbert Rowse Armstrong, who poisoned a wife, and possibly a business partner, before he offered arsenic-laced scones to a rival attorney and his murderous ways were detected. He was hanged at Gloucester on May 31, 1922.

Burke and Hare were the Edinburgh body snatchers who killed their lodgers and sold the bodies to Dr. Knox at the medical school for dissection. Like the other killers mentioned in Wimsey's discourse, these two were caught when they pushed their luck and murdered Daft Jamie, a popular town character. His body was recognized by the medical students, and the body snatchers were subsequently arrested. It was their sixteenth murder. Burke was hanged in Edinburgh on January 28, 1829.

It is significant that all the examples of real crimes mentioned in *Unnatural Death* are medical-related or poisoning murders, because the murderer Wimsey and Parker are pursuing in the novel is a nurse who kills by lethal injection.

The Documents in the Case, the nonseries epistolary novel that Sayers coauthored with Robert Eustace, contains the usual references to actual murderers to bolster the characters' philosophical discussion of crime. In the Statement of John Munting (Item 37), the novelist Munting recalls a conversation that he had with Harwood Lathom about the artist's preference for lodgings in a nonfashionable district rather than in arty Chelsea. Lathom insists that the suburbs are the last bastion of reality. Artists believe in nothing, he says; but the middle class, obsessed with respectability and keeping up appearances, will persecute and die for their bourgeois beliefs. "Look at Crippen," Lathom says. "Look at Bywaters. Look at the man who hid his dead wife in a bath and ate his meals on the lid for fear that somebody should suspect a scandal."

All three of the cases cited by Lathom involve murders committed in connection with adultery, which is appropriate, because in the novel Lathom poisons the husband of his mistress. All three of the murderers he mentioned lived in respectable middle-class suburbs of London. H. H. Crippen, a mild-mannered doctor, poisoned his domineering wife with hyoscine in 1910 and buried her headless body in the basement of his house off the Camden road in North London. He then fled for Canada on an ocean liner, the *Montrose*, accompanied by his mistress, Ethel LeNeve, who was disguised as a boy. A wireless message alerted the captain to Crippen's presence aboard, and he was apprehended by Scotland Yard Inspector Walter Dew, who overtook the *Montrose* on a faster ship. Crippen pleaded guilty to the murder of his wife but insisted that Ethel LeNeve was not an accomplice. She was acquitted; he was hanged at Pentonville Prison on November 23, 1910. It is odd that Crippen should be such a famous murderer that his name has passed into the language as a synonym for monster. So mild is his crime by modern standards of depravity that if he had committed it yesterday instead of in 1910, he would be relegated to a small article on the back page of the newspaper.

Frederick Bywaters, a ship's writer with the P&O Line, fell in love with a married woman named Edith Thompson, and the two wrote long, passionate letters to each other while Bywaters was on a voyage to the Far East. When he returned from sea on October 3, 1922, Bywaters stabbed Thompson's husband in a London alley, while Edith shrieked for help for the dying man. Both lovers were subsequently arrested and tried for murder. Thompson's letters had been full of fanciful tales of putting glass into her husband's food and urging Bywaters to "do something desperate." Despite Bywaters's insistence that his mistress had not incited him to the crime, both were convicted of Percy Thompson's murder, and they were hanged at their respective London prisons on January 9, 1923.

The man who "hid his dead wife in a bath and ate his meals on the lid" apparently refers to Cecil Maltby, a London tailor, who murdered his live-in mistress, Alice Hilda Middleton. In August 1922 Alice Middleton disappeared; she was reported missing in December when her husband, a merchant seaman, returned from the Far East. When the police went to question Maltby, he refused to let them into his shop, claiming that Alice had left him in August. In January the police obtained a health order authorizing them to break into Maltby's premises. As they smashed in the door they heard a single shot and found Maltby dying of a self-inflicted gunshot wound. The decomposing body of Alice Middleton was found in the kitchen bath, wrapped in a sheet. Notes in Maltby's handwriting were scattered about the apartment, attesting to the fact that Alice had been dead since August and that her lover had kept her body there with him for the following four months, until the forced entry of the police gave him the impetus to commit suicide.

The Thompson and Bywaters case echoes the fictional crime within *The Documents in the Case*: the murder of an older husband by his wife's lover. The cases of Crippen and Maltby are lesser reflections of the situation: a love triangle in suburbia resulting in the death of one of the principals.

Dorothy Sayers was never particularly interested in the mechanics of true crime. She seemed to concoct her plots, replete with ciphers and esoteric information, as puzzles for intellectual readers. With the probable exception of *Strong Poison*, she did not try to fictionalize actual cases, nor did she worry about imitating reality. Sayers was concerned with taxing the wits of the reader, and with conveying philosophical opinions within the text. Her knowledge of crime seems superficial: the sort of information collected by any intelligent person who knows history and follows current events. Each true case cited in a Sayers novel is one that the readers of her time would recognize without explanation, and these crimes are always chosen to echo the concocted plot of the novel. Mentioning actual cases bolsters the impression that Wimsey and Parker are genuine detectives who take a professional interest in crime. Sayers could quote murder for her purpose, but scripture was more in her line.

The Art of Framing Lies

Dorothy L. Sayers on Mystery Fiction

AARON ELKINS

In a famous tour de force called "Aristotle on Detective Fiction," Dorothy Sayers set down the wisest, most succinct piece of advice on writing mysteries ever to find its way into print.

> The art of framing lies—but mark! of framing lies in *the right way*. . . . There is the crux. Any fool can tell a lie, and any fool can believe it; but the right method is to tell the *truth* in such a way that the *intelligent* reader is seduced into telling the lie for himself. That the writer himself should tell a flat lie is contrary to all the canons of detective art.

Since I first came across it almost a decade ago, this sage and insightful counsel has been the closest thing I have to a guiding principle, and I sometimes wonder how I managed to stumble through my first few mysteries without it. Nowadays it helps me avoid (or, more likely, climb back out of) a dozen pitfalls, maybe more, in every book. If it isn't quite All You Need to Know About How to Write a Mystery, it's as near as anything has ever been, and it's not a bad start on All You Need to Know About How to Read a Mystery either.

Sayers wrote those words in 1936 (generously giving credit to Aristotle for the original thought), and they appeared in a series of fascinating essays on the mystery that Sayers published from 1928 to 1936. These essays offer insights into Sayers's views on detective fiction that are more personal and direct than the ones we get from reading her novels and stories—a view through her own eyes, so to speak, rather than the eyes of Lord Peter or Montague Egg, discerning though they may be.

This centenary year, with so much interest focused on Dorothy Sayers, seems like a good time to haul some of her essays out, dust them off, and see what they tell us about her, about her books, and about the time in which she wrote.

And maybe a little bit more about just what made her mysteries so extraordinary.

CHRISTIE *v.* DOSTOEVSKI

Writing in the early 1930s, Sayers warned of "an increased solemnity" in the field of detective fiction. "Mystery mongering has become self-conscious," she tells us doomfully, then pauses and delivers the chilling cruncher: "Monographs and critical studies are appearing."

I think it's safe to assume that her tongue was wedged firmly in her cheek when she wrote this, because she herself was the first great critic of mystery fiction. At a time when her fellow mystery mongers were spending their spare time formulating the "laws" of detective writing—the ten commandments of Monsignor Ronald Knox, the twenty rules of S. S. Van Dine, the locked-room-murder dictums of John Dickson Carr (as told by Dr. Gideon Fell), Sayers was virtually alone in exploring the literary aspects of the mystery, its artistic status, and its place in the past and future history of the novel.

Her hopes for it weren't what one would call impossibly high. In 1928 she concluded flatly that the detective story "does not, and by hypothesis never can, attain the loftiest level of literary attainment." Her reasoning, in a nutshell, was that to *be* a detective story, a mystery must concentrate on detection. It cannot show us the inner workings of the murderer's mind (she was to change her view on this a few years later) because then the identity of the murderer would be given away; and it cannot probe in depth the powerful and deep-seated emotions that envelop the crime of murder in the real world. The mystery, she felt, was no place for Dostoevskian dissections of the passions. "A too violent emotion flung into the glittering mechanism of the detective story jars the movement by disturbing its delicate balance."

But three years later the mechanism was showing signs of tarnish, and Sayers did an about-face. "There has recently been a reaction against the extremely mathematical form of detective problem which held the field for so long," she says in 1931. She was convinced that the cunning puzzle-stories of the teens and twenties, with their ingenious but unrealistic murder methods, their outlandish plot convolutions, and their contrived, near-mathematical solutions, had worn out their welcome.

The reading public, she believed, had had their fill of stories that were more than clever enough in plot but were prosaically told, devoid of depth, and peopled with infallible detectives and other one-dimensional, predictable stock characters. "It is evident that there is a genuine eagerness to bring the detective story into line with the traditions of the English novel and to make it increasingly a real part of literature," she writes hopefully (and maybe a little wistfully).

Just how widespread that "genuine eagerness" was is open to question—you'd certainly never know it was there from looking at the mystery fiction being published at the time—but there is no question about Sayers's commitment to improving the mystery's artistic status. Mysteries had become overintellectualized, she complained. The "mechanical ingenuities" (formerly known as "glittering mechanisms") had become all-important, so much so that they had all but buried the treatment of social and psychological themes that are at the heart of any serious literature.

Without that concern, she felt that the mystery's future was in doubt. "No kind of fiction can survive for very long cut off from the great interests of humanity and from the main stream of contemporary literature," she tells us soberly. Mysteries had to change their spots or go the way of the Restoration tragedy. But she stuck to her guns on the matter of emotions; detective stories were not the place to analyze or expand on the great human passions.

So what did she have in mind? Certainly not, she made plain, the way of the "modern" novel. In fact, she had some rather unkind things to say about "the kind of modern novel which, beginning at the end, rambles backwards and forwards without particular direction and ends on an indeterminate note, and for no ascertainable reason except the publisher's refusal to provide more printing and paper for seven-and-sixpence." Mysteries, by contrast, were to be solidly and logically constructed, with a clear beginning, middle, and end. So declared Sayers, once again bringing in Aristotle to back her up. Experimental fiction? Stream-of-consciousness? Don't even think about it, she said—or words to that effect.

What, then? In what way could the mystery develop that would make it more profound as literature, yet allow it to retain the very attributes that defined it? Curiously enough, she felt that the most promising direction was not forward but back "to the Victorian conception of a detective story that should at the same time be a novel of character and manners." More curious still, that's precisely the path mystery fiction did take, and is still on, or so it looks from where I sit.

Today's mysteries, both English and American, are chock-full of the keenest observations and interpretations of social behavior; they are novels of manners in the classic sense of the term. Private-eye novels, police-procedurals, academics, cozies (terms unknown in Sayers's day)—all derive a very large part of their appeal from the detailed and perceptive ways in which their authors depict the norms and traditions of society in general, and especially of the particular segments of society they write about.

As readers we enjoy the realistic cop talk, or the academic politics, or the small-town folkways as much as, or more than, those intricate details of plot construction that mystery writers rack their brains to come up with. In my view, it's the mystery—surely not mainstream fiction—that has picked up where Jane Austen and Anthony Trollope and John Galsworthy and Arnold Bennett left off.

The funny part is, Dorothy Sayers not only predicted this as a critic; as a novelist she was instrumental in bringing it to pass. Nowadays we tend to think of her books as exemplifying the classic tradition of the mystery, but that is selling her short. Actually she was following her own injunction and plowing new ground, one of the very few writers of her time departing from the traditional detective story approach of Freeman Wills Crofts, Eden Phillpotts, S. S. Van Dine, and even, for the most part, Agatha Christie. Or maybe it was old ground. In any case, she was writing novels of a sort that hadn't been seen since Victorian times—since *The Moonstone*, to be precise—that combined the best qualities of the conventional detective story with a genuinely novelistic attention to the depiction and exploration of mores, manners, and attitudes.

Those of us in the mystery-mongering business today, and therefore necessarily in her shadow, have been trying, with greater or lesser degrees of success, to do the same thing ever since.

PLAYING FAIR

The rules of fair play (the term is hers) were very close to Sayers's heart. You can see it in her novels, and you can see it in her essays. She meant by it just what we mean today: detectives must "display their clues to the reader as soon as they have picked them up." No fair hiding anything and saving it for the finale to astound and bedazzle the reader with the detective's sagacity, as Conan Doyle, then at the end of his writing career, had brilliantly done for so many years, and others, less brilliantly—and less successfully—along with him.

That would no longer do, Sayers said. When a detective finds, say, "a small, blue object" not far from the murdered man, he'd better not slip it into his pocket without letting the reader have a good look, too. "Connoisseurs have come, more and more, to call for a story which puts them on an equal footing with the detective himself, as regards all clues and discoveries."

The fair play rule, she told us in 1936, had gradually become "the test of quality . . . the most important principle of the modern detective story." And she expected reader discrimination on this point to increase with time.

She was right. What was then a test of quality has today become a given, one so accepted that it's hardly worth mentioning. Yes, some writers play a little more fair than others, but any of us who dared to make a practice of keeping a few little things up our detective's sleeves for the denouement would be drummed out of the corps by reviewers and readers both, and rightly so. No significant omissions, if you please, no cover-ups, and definitely no lies. (On the other hand, to "tell the *truth* in such a way that the *intelligent* reader is seduced into telling the lie for himself . . . ," well, that's another thing altogether.)

Sayers also had an ancillary principle that hasn't held up quite so well: "The detective story," she instructs us, "seeks to leave nothing unexplained." But it seems to me that readers, and editors too, have become more forgiving in this regard. Life is not, we feel, arranged in tidy packages with every loose end tied up, so why should we insist on having every last red herring cleared up at the end of a mystery novel?

Speaking for myself, I'm of two minds about this. On the one hand, I do like to find every separate loose end neatly tied up at the end of a book; I feel better for it. On the other, I must say that I don't mind being spared those interminable get-'em-all-together-in-the-drawing-room, wrap-up-every-detail disquisitions with which so many otherwise wonderful old mysteries feebly petered out.

Sayers could manage those harangues—most of the time—with verve and wit. Not many others could.

Not all of Sayers's predictions turned out to be on the mark or even close to it. (After sixty years, whose do?) Here, for curiosity's sake, are a couple that failed to pan out.

THE CRIMINAL MIND

In the 1920s, with the infant science of psychology beginning to fire the public imagination, it seemed reasonable to expect that new insights into the criminal mind would provide a rich lode for the detective writer to mine. Sayers pointed with approval to several recent books in which actual murder cases had been fictionalized.

And she commended Francis Iles's *Malice Aforethought*, which she described as a study in murder as opposed to a conventional detective story. "Before very long," Sayers predicted hopefully, "a formula for combining the two types of story will be discovered by somebody."

Well, it was, but not until 1966, and it didn't turn out to be a fictionalized murder but a nonfiction novel: Truman Capote's *In Cold Blood*. Sayers was right—it was a stunning hit—but it didn't have much effect on the mystery. What followed from it, after a time, was what has become an avalanche of true-crime books, with their roots in journalism, not in fiction—and especially not in detective fiction.

So Sayers had this one wrong. For better or worse, with occasional exceptions, mystery writers have continued to put their focus where it's been since Edgar Allan Poe started it all—on the mind and personality of the detective, not of the murderer.

WOMEN AND MURDER

Interestingly, Sayers did not look favorably on the potential of women as fictional detectives. "In order to justify their choice of sex," she wrote in 1928, "they are obliged to be so irritatingly intuitive as to destroy that quiet enjoyment of the logical which we look for in our detective reading. . . . Marriage, also, looms too large in their view of life."

She was, of course, reflecting the culture of her time, but it was her personal view as well. She just didn't see much place for women as detectives, although she did allow that they might do better—a little bit better—as amateur sleuths than as professionals.

If nothing else, this point of view by the most eminent mystery writer of her time, and a woman at that, and a feminist at that, is a reminder of how things have changed. Women, it turns out, make pretty fair cops and private eyes after all. Marriage, looming large or not (and usually it's not in today's books), doesn't seem to get in the way after all. I'm sure that if she were still around, Sayers would be delighted to have been proven wrong.

Along related lines, she muttered misanthropically about "love interest," which she described as a "fettering convention from which detective fiction is only slowly freeing itself. . . . The less love in a detective story," she tells us irritably, "the better."

Unexpected words from the creator of Harriet Vane, the woman who was to cause Peter Wimsey all the woes (and a few of the joys) of passionate love while he pursued her for five long years (from 1930 to 1935) and three long books, before she finally yielded on the very last page—the very last line—of *Gaudy Night*.

Well, nobody can claim to be totally consistent, and most of us are glad that Sayers followed her fictional instincts, not her own critical and unromantic prescription.

And I am happy to report that love interest in mysteries remains alive and well.

DOROTHY SAYERS LETS ONE GET BY

Once in a great while, Sayers failed to spot the start of an important trend, and one that she missed entirely is what we might call the pedagogical novel, for want of a better term. Today, readers who like to learn things while they read (and mystery buffs generally do) can get expert guidance in an astonishing variety of subjects ranging from the practical to the highly esoteric. There are mysteries that offer a semester's worth of education in Egyptology, art, medicine (forensic and other), child psychology, antiques, horse racing, dentistry, accounting, Indian culture, law, Catholicism, Judaism (Reform and Orthodox), anthropology (cultural and physical), and sailing. Indeed, there are entire *series* dealing in depth with each of these subjects, and they are among the most popular in the field.

This rewarding trend can trace its existence to Dorothy Sayers herself, and no further. True, mysteries have a long and delightful history of presenting scientific and esoteric information, right on back to Poe. But it is one thing to furnish the reader with an isolated fact or two that the detective lets drop about the rate at which an 0.04 percent solution of beclomethasone dipropionate is absorbed into the bloodstream—and another thing entirely to present a thoroughly researched, coherent body of information about an entire field of knowledge (and something else yet again to make it an integral, absorbing, and necessary part of the mystery).

Yet that is exactly what she did with campanology (of all things) in *The Nine Tailors*, and detective fiction has never been the same. How curious that Sayers, with her wealth of critical, perceptive writing on the mystery field, and her many calls to improve it, never seemed to recognize that she herself had set the pattern for what was to become one of the most productive and popular currents in the genre.

I thought it was high time somebody thanked her for it.

Dorothy L. Sayers
on Dante

ANNE PERRY

Why did Dorothy Sayers choose to translate Dante's *Divine Comedy*? She had been a highly successful mystery writer for years and cannot have needed either the money or the recognition. Perhaps less well known, she was also a playwright, a poet, and a medieval scholar, having graduated from Oxford with first-class honors. Was it her love of all these that prompted her? The twilight of the medieval world and the dawn of the Renaissance is surely one of the most exciting times in the history of man, and one of the most fundamental to Western culture and thought. What place is more central than Florence? Is there a greater pivotal figure than Dante Alighieri, or a more profound, all-encompassing, and seminal work than the *Divine Comedy*?

And then there is the challenge of translating any poetry. One must weigh the relative merits of the literal meaning of the words, as far as they can be translated from one language and culture into another, against the emotional flavor of the word or phrase, its color, its sound on the tongue, and its rhythm, and the necessity of rhyme. One must not forget humor or double meaning where these are intended (of which Dante is very fond), and yet it is a disaster where they are not! In her long and totally necessary introductions DLS explains in many instances why she chose the words or phrases she did, and gives us alternative readings with which to compare them.

She also gives us an illuminating sketch of the life and personality of Dante himself, without which the whole work would be robbed of much of its meaning. All the way through, her notes on each canto are not only interesting and highly readable, but are fundamental to understanding the allegories and symbols. And she writes so fluently it is easy to enjoy, even if taken separately from the text. Her comments are acutely satisfying and thought provoking and infinitely enriching to the work.

To illustrate Sayers's remarkable work, let us look more closely at her translation of "Hell," the first and most popular part of the *Divine Comedy*. We begin in the dark wood, symbolic of life itself, where Dante is lost. "The mere breath of memory stirs the old fear in the blood." Already we are gripped with the vividness and the power of the words. Here he meets with the three beasts who stand for the three categories of sins. First is the leopard of incontinence, or self-indulgence, which Dante describes simply as "di pel maculato era coverta"—literally, "covered with a spotted hide." But DLS captures the lyricism and surface charm and lightness of self-indulgence by saying "clothed in a fine furred pelt all dapple-dyed." This is a single example of a myriad happy translations less literal but perhaps catching a truer essence of the spirit and the emotional impact of the poet's vision.

Next Dante meets the lion of the sins of anger, and last the ravening wolf of the deepest sins, those involving the intellect, peculiarly the gift of man: malice and fraud, the perversion of that which should have been good, the betrayals.

He meets Virgil, who symbolizes human wisdom and virtue without the aid of the divine grace that alone brings redemption. There is far more to all Dante's symbols than there is room here to explore, nor would it be appropriate, but DLS opens vista after vista, and leads one to the brink of limitless new thought. I can only try to give a sufficient taste to tempt you to the rest.

Above the gates of hell are inscribed the words that have passed into our culture (I even saw them quoted in a Fred Basset cartoon in the newspaper!). DLS translates them as, "Lay down all hope, you that go in by me." It is the one cavil I have with her. I still prefer the old "Abandon hope, all ye who enter here."

With some wonderfully poetic descriptions of chaos, Dante and Virgil pass the vestibule, where dwell the spirits of those who never made a clear choice in life but forever hedged their bets and havered without commitment, the moral cowards, the lukewarm. Again DLS's notes make plain what is somewhat concealed in poetic imagery.

After passing the first river of hell, Acheron, the joyless, they enter into the first circle of hell itself, and limbo, "the dolorous chasm of the Pit, ringing with infinite groans like gathered thunder." Limbo is where the unbaptized dwell with no torment save exclusion from the presence of God.

They descend past Minos, the judge of hell, "holding his ghastly sessions," into the first circle of incontinence. They meet many famous adulterers and speak to Francesca da Rimini. DLS's commentary here is among the best of all her remarks. It is one of the clearest descriptions of the nature of sin I have met with. The lovers are borne on a black wind, "the blast of hell that never rests from whirling," which symbolizes the passions that tore away all balance and decision in the world, which in hell are a permanent state. It is a vivid way of showing how we are punished not *for* our sins, but *by* them. All the light charm is stripped away, and the sin is seen in its nakedness, "a howling darkness of helpless discomfort." The punishment is the sin lived forever, without the illusion that charmed and deceived us in life. Perhaps the most profound lesson of the entire work is that hell is never a punishment inflicted from outside, but always the soul's own deliberate choice.

This is elaborated throughout all the circles of hell down to the deepest, the grades of sin explained as one descends from mutual self-indulgence through solitary appetite to indulgence at the expense of others; then through the sins of anger and violence to those of the mind and the heart, the treacheries against all that is good, the perversion of trust and destruction not only of man but of the very nature of good itself.

In the next circle are the gluttonous. As DLS tells us, these feed their appetite alone, degraded from mutual indulgence to solitary vice. In her words gluttony is a "cold sensuality, a sodden and filthy spiritual wretchedness." This is indeed robbing it of its outward appearance of jollity and innocence, and showing us its real nature. The gluttons sit forever in icy mud beneath a driving rain.

Below this circle is that of the hoarders and spendthrifts. One might at first wonder why Dante should condemn them so bitterly, but DLS explains how solitary indulgence has now declined to the enraged awareness of the incompatible appetites of others. Indifference has become mutual antagonism. Here on the surface of the morass each sinner attacks the other in a frenzy of rage, while below in the wretched depths snarl those sullen self-haters who are so choked with incoherent fury they can utter no sense. Sayers shows us clearly the parallels not only to individual appetite but to the political disintegration of the community and the essentially selfish nature of the sin.

Virgil then leads Dante down a steep cliff to the second river of hell, the Styx, which means "hateful"; it is the boundary between upper and nether hell. It is a stagnant marsh of slime in which wallow the wrathful, the fourth sin of incontinence.

At the far side they come to the city of Dis, before whose red-hot walls Virgil seeks entrance and for the first time is repulsed. For once his command is refused. DLS explains that this symbolizes humanism's bafflement by the deliberate will to do evil. It is something beyond the understanding of even the wisest.

A most interesting event occurs in this canto (8). One of the wrathful appeals to Dante, crying out to him, and Dante repels him and shrinks away. Virgil praises him for this, which seems at first to be a pitiless and unchristian reaction. DLS points out that in hell the soul is eternally fixed in the pattern of behavior it has chosen, in this case furious anger. Therefore it cannot now enjoy that which it has rejected. Dante's reaction is a reflection of what this sin is, and Dante realizes its true horror, and also something he has not apparently perceived before, that it is immeasurably dangerous! In a similar parallel, Francesca da Rimini woke in Dante a mirroring reaction. The easy pity and shallow warmth that were in her the beginning of her fall to indulgence, stirred in him only a facile sympathy, soon passing.

The gluttonous call forth little pity because they feel little. The wrathful elected cruelty and pleasure in others' pain; therefore they perceive all others as equally cruel and can no longer recognize good even when they meet it.

Divine help is needed to obtain entrance to Dis and the whole depth of nether hell. In this canto there are verses of wonderful poetry so fine I find myself reading and rereading them for their rhythm, vitality, and marvelous descriptions. Frogs go "squattering" over the pond. "Whole shoals of ruined souls" scatter before the heavenly messenger who comes "walking the water of Styx with unwet feet."

When the messenger departs, Virgil and Dante are on a plain with the open and burning tombs of heretics. Dante meets one of the many historical figures he refers to; DLS explained them in more detail either in the notes or in the glossary. The *Inferno* is frequently highly political, both on the local scale of Florentine politics of the period, and as an example of political life in general and the nature of all community. But Dante certainly did not shrink from placing many of his personal enemies in whatever circle of hell he considered appropriate. He also included much prophecy about what would happen both to Florence and to himself.

Here DLS explains that by heretics Dante did not mean the unbelieving, or those of other faiths, but those who understood faith and deliberately, by act of will, denied trust or obedience. They are the "intellectually obdurate," the deliberately arrogant of soul.

In canto 11 they descend to the seventh circle, and Virgil explains to Dante the whole plan of hell, the degrees of sin as they go deeper and deeper to the smallest circle, the throne of Satan himself. The notes give an interesting explanation of the three sins punished in the third ring of the lion, those of violence: sodomy, usury, and blasphemy. This choice needs some light thrown upon it, which DLS does with startling relevance, lifting the immediacy from 1300 and bringing it to today.

Sodomy is self-explanatory, as the waste of the fruitfulness of man's own body. More interestingly, usury is violence against the order of productivity, of which there are only two sources: nature, or the earth; and art, or man's labor. Usury is a contortion, or twisting, so that something naturally sterile, money, is made to breed at the expense of the truly productive. And since the earth is God's, this is also a violence against God. This is one of the many political points that are acutely modern. Dante died in 1321, DLS in 1957. One cannot help wondering what either of them would have made of our present exploitation of the earth's finite resources and our pollution of its seas and atmosphere, the obesity of many in the Western world while the third world starves! In which circle of hell would Dante have placed profiteers?

Perhaps this is a suitable place to appreciate how thought provoking and worthwhile is the whole concept of sin, its nature and interrelation, and its effect upon the spirit of man.

No matter how engrossed you are in Dante's poetry and narrative, DLS's commentary must surely waken in you speculation on your own hierarchy of sinners. Are there any new sins? It is nearly seven hundred years since Dante wrote. He lived nearly two centuries before Columbus and before the rise of the Spanish Inquisition. Industrialization was hundreds of years in the future; slums and ghettos, the machine age, the flight from the land to cities were all undreamed. Even the Black Death lay in the future. The Renaissance was still only a faint glimmer of dawn on the margin of the mind. World war, systematic scientific genocide were beyond the power of intellect to conceive.

Or are all sins merely facets of self-indulgence, violence and fraud of one sort or another, simply wearing different guises, the same body in an up-to-date dress? Do the wagers of world war belong in Dante's Phlegethon, the river of boiling blood, the third great waterway of hell? Do the propagandists who blind whole nations and deceive peoples belong in the last pit of Cocytus, the frozen lake at the bottom of hell where all the movement of body or soul is ended?

Across Phlegethon, Dante and Virgil come to the pathless forest of withered and bleeding trees that are the bodies of suicides. Here they are attacked by harpies, half human, half birds, ravening with a hunger that can never be satisfied. These creatures swoop on food, tearing it apart and defiling it so it is unusable. They are the image of the will to destroy, as suicides have destroyed their bodies.

The medieval church, and indeed the Renaissance and modern churches until very lately, regarded suicide as self-hatred and a mortal sin. Since man is made in the image of God, this makes it also a blasphemy. (The Victorians sometimes went so far as to revive an attempted suicide in order to hang them!)

However, we have come to a gentler wisdom, recognizing that despair can spring from many causes that are not sinful, simply tragic. Disease of mind or body, mental agony arising from abuse, and many other causes we do not understand may lead to a self-loathing or an inability to endure any longer that we do not condemn. Perhaps had Dante seen our age he might have consigned many suicides to purgatory, where they could have worked out their salvation, and even assigned some to a higher fate; surely few would have been beyond his compassion. Maybe consuming self-pity would be better suited to this desolation, where the trees exude blood when torn and are denied even human shape.

Now Virgil and Dante proceed to a desert of burning sand where it perpetually rains fire. Here lie those who blasphemed against God. They lie on their backs eternally staring up at the heaven they defied.

Next after the bloody stream, the sterile wood, and the burning sands, they came again to the banks of Phlegethon and the edge of a far greater abyss. Here are the sodomites, condemned to run forever facing the human body against which they offended, wasting and perverting its natural function. Curiously, one of these was Brunetto Latini, Dante's old tutor, whom he obviously still regards with affection and gratitude for the past.

DLS speculates in the notes to this canto (15) that in the circle of those violent against their own bodies, Dante might have placed drug abusers and the vicious type of alcoholics. No doubt Dante would have known alcohol and its dangers, but such things as cocaine and heroin would be unknown to him, and certainly the modern drugs like crack and angel dust were probably unknown even to DLS.

The next canto brings Dante and Virgil to the edge of the abyss and the deepest of the three great divisions of hell, where are consigned those who committed the sins of the wolf. First are the sins of malice simple: panderers and seducers, flatterers, sorcerers, hypocrites, counselors of fraud, and sowers of discord. Last and deepest of all, beyond the well of the giants, who symbolize mere primitive urge, lie the sins of malice complex: those who betrayed.

There is an immense waterfall plunging over the brink where all the rivers of hell empty into the chasm, with apparently no way of passing it. Virgil takes from Dante his girdle. DLS says this is possibly a symbol of chastity now no longer necessary. We have passed from the incontinent sins of youth and the flesh, to the more profound sins of the mind and of the soul. She points out that this is only one of several possible interpretations, but it is a consistent allegory.

Virgil casts the girdle into the void, and presently a hideous creature flies upward. It is Geryon, its features a combination of human, bestial, and reptilian. It represents the duplicitous nature of fraud, with the face of an honest man and the soul of a beast.

While Virgil is talking with this creature, Dante observes the usurers, "sitting on the sand, on the empty edge of space," looking upon the ground forever, huge purses strung about their necks, because they sinned against nature by making money breed, instead of the earth. DLS points out that they may be taken to represent all civilizations that multiply material luxuries at the expense of the necessities of life. There is the opening for endless political and economic thought on this!

Geryon takes Dante and Virgil upon his back and swoops down the abyss into the deepest circle of nether hell and the sins of the wolf. Here we come to the Malbowges, or evil trenches, where dwell those who committed malicious frauds upon mankind in general. Here, flogged and goaded by demons, are the panderers and procurers who sold others' bodies for the uses of lust. DLS does not suggest it, but will perhaps all manner of pornographers be here also? Dante places the seducers in this ditch, both male and female. Lastly are the flatterers, steeped in perpetual ordure. They are vividly described "and heard them cough, and slap themselves with their hands, and snuffle and spit," evoking the eternal filth of those who pervert the use of language and respect.

DLS's comments on this canto are so thought provoking and her perceptions so intense that I would like simply to reproduce them all, but that would be inappropriate. She sees the successive Malbowges as peculiarly the image of social corruption and the progressive disintegration of every type of community relationship. All the media of human exchange are perverted and falsified till nothing remains but the descent into the last void where all trust is eternally annihilated. Fraud is the abuse of the peculiarly human faculty of reason, and the demons as personified now represent perverted intellect rather than mere appetites.

We begin with those who deliberately exploited the passions and weaknesses of others in order to make tools of people to serve their own ends. In the second Malbowge are the flatterers (interestingly, a trifle lower—the corruption of the mind being marginally more depraved than the corruption of the body). These wallow in perpetual excrement. They abused and defiled language, the communication between one mind and another. DLS notes, "Dante did not live to see the full development of political propaganda, commercial advertisement and sensational journalism, but he had prepared a place for them!"

In the third Malbowge we find simoniacs, head downward in fiery pits, those who sold holy offices and sacraments. They subordinated heavenly things to the earthly; therefore they themselves are forever reversed. DLS notes this is a far wider allegory than simply the sale of indulgences or livings. She says, "A mercenary marriage, for example, is also the sale of a sacrament." A disturbing thought! Presumably by extension so would be a marriage made for rank, professional advancement, or any other personal gain. Perhaps also in this torment belong those who profess or teach a faith they do not believe, in order to be paid for it—which opens up a very wide field in today's material and gullible world. I wonder what DLS would have said of some present-day preachers!

In the fourth Malbowge are sorcerers, here meant as those who strive to foretell the future. These are so twisted that their faces are to the rear, and they are compelled forever to walk backward, their own bodies distorted. They typify the twisting of knowledge through magical arts to dominate the environment and, worse, the personalities of others, robbing them of their free will. DLS includes in this sin the attempt at conditioning the minds of others and manipulating them for power or gain. That opens up vast areas of thought and speculation. How sure are any of us that our attempts to guide are free from arrogance and the twisted sin of unrighteous dominion?

In the fifth Malbowge, plunged in boiling pitch, are barrators, those who sold public office for money. As DLS points out, they are not mere sellers of position but of justice itself. When they are seen in this way, it is not hard to understand why they should be relegated to so low a place. Demons are shown quarreling among themselves, violent, cruel, and full of trickery and deceit. There is no love, no cooperation, no common cause in hell. The devil is the master of chaos.

In the sixth Malbowge we find the hypocrites, weighed down by cloaks of gold—lined with lead, "a weary mantle for eternity." One remembers that of all things, Christ could not abide a hypocrite.

Here Caiaphas is crucified on the ground. Again I would quote DLS directly: "The condition in this life of the man who sacrifices his inner truth to expediency." How passionately immediate is Dante, yet how universal!

Canto 24 begins with lyrical poetry:

> *What time the Sun in the year's early youth,*
> *Beneath Aquarius rinses his bright hair,*
> *And nights begin to dwindle toward the south.*

Just in case we forget, DLS is also a poet, translating one of the great epic poems of mankind.

The following two Malbowges are devoted to thieves, whose crime was regarded immeasurably more seriously in medieval society than now. DLS explains this fully, telling us how at that time a man's property was considered an extension of his being. It prompts thoughts of the independence of those who have not the means to sustain themselves, and the griefs and sins that may follow this, the myriad subjugations of others, the coercions and seductions. Perhaps this is the right end for exploiters and enslavers who rob people of the rewards of their labor.

In the eighth Malbowge, consumed in the "thievish fire," are counselors to fraud, those spiritual thieves who robbed men of their integrity. In the ninth, the sowers of discord are hacked to pieces by the sundering sword, then the flesh reunites, to be again hewn apart. Three types are exemplified: those who fomented religious schism, those who sowed civil strife, and those who caused family disunity. They are in this circle of fraud because they deceived others into seeing their own twisted view of the world, "ready to rip the whole fabric of society to gratify a sectional egotism."

Dante and Virgil drop still farther to the tenth and last Malbowge, where the falsifiers are stricken with fearful diseases. Again, to our modern understanding this may seem an extraordinarily vile condemnation for a very moderate sin. But DLS explains brilliantly. These are not merely alchemists, but "every kind of deceiver who tampers with the basic commodities by which society lives — the adulterers of food and drugs," etc. This paints an entirely different picture, one full of endless suffering! Can there be much that is more despicable than the adulteration of medicines, the poisoning of food or the atmosphere, for profit? Perhaps in this trench there may be a place for those who sell for profit drugs that will bring ruin and death to the users.

The Valley of Disease is an image of a society that acknowledges no obligation to any honor or faith among fellow men. Now every medium of exchange or communication has been corrupted and falsified, every identity is a lie, nothing certain remains, nothing can be trusted. In the next canto we find specific falsifiers, impersonators (who pervert identity), perjurers (who pervert words), and forgers of money. Society has descended to chaos. Nothing at all is what it seems; truth itself has gone.

Dante and Virgil have now come to the end of the Malbowges and are at the edge of the well at the floor of the abyss. Here, sunk to the waist in the ice, are the giants who represent the primal urges, blind and shorn of any intelligence or love to redeem them. They are the pride of Satan which rebelled against God, although they have the classical names of Greek antiquity. Nimrod is braggart stupidity, Ephialtes senseless rage, and Antaeus brainless vanity. "One may call them the doom of nonsense, violence and triviality, overtaking a civilisation in which the whole natural order is abrogated."

Having climbed down their huge bodies, Dante and Virgil are now in the region of fraud complex, the Pit of Treachery, the frozen lake of Cocytus, the River of Mourning, the last waterway of hell. This again is divided into four parts: Caina is for those who betrayed their kindred; they are plunged to their necks in ice. Antenora is for those who betrayed their country; they are frozen two by two in one hole, eternally gnawing at each other's heads. Ptolomea is for those who betrayed their guests; they are alone in the utter cold of damnation. And lowest of all is Judecca for those who have betrayed their lords; they are totally submerged in the everlasting ice.

Beneath the fires of hell, the burning and turmoil and clamor, is the frozen and eternal silence of the lost soul. This is the final state of sin: ice cold, immobile, and alone. Surely this is living death.

After Judecca, Virgil leads Dante through the passage in the earth toward Mount Purgatory, which is in the southern hemisphere (interestingly, in 1300 Dante has no doubt that the earth is round!), and he "came forth to look once more upon the stars"—a wiser, humbler man. Such a journey through hell must surely "harrow and beautify thy soul," a quotation I cannot place but which is so appropriate I make no apology for using it.

To answer my question, Why did Dorothy Sayers choose to translate Dante? there are countless reasons. She has written her translation with such lyricism, such perception and clarity, that I am richer and wiser for having read it, as I shall be every time I read it again. I shall continue to be enlightened, charmed by vision and beauty, moved to deeper thought, and rededicated to attempting a better life. What more could any writer ask of their work? Thank you, Dorothy Sayers.

Unsoothing Sayers

RALPH McINERNY

In dedicating the *Paradiso* to Can Grande della Scala, one of the patrons who made a long exile from his native Florence tolerable, Dante tells us that his poem is literally about the state of souls after death, but its allegorical meaning is the way in which human beings, by the exercise of their free will, earn fitting punishment or reward. Dorothy Sayers alludes to this in the introduction to her translation of the *Comedy* when she instructs her reader on what it takes to understand Dante.

> We must abandon any idea that we are the slaves of chance, or environment, or our subconscious; any vague notion that good and evil are merely relative terms, or that conduct and opinion do not really matter; any comfortable persuasion that, however shiftlessly we muddle through life, it will somehow or other come out all right.

Her readers will not need to be told that her own mysteries would be unintelligible apart from that same view of life.

Maybe all mysteries would be.

Maybe fiction generally. Flannery O'Connor thought so, asserting that *all* literature must have an anagogic meaning, a meaning beyond the literal narration of imaginary events.

Dorothy Sayers's magnificent translation—alas, unfinished—of *The Divine Comedy* raises the question of the relationship between that endeavor and her mystery fiction. The translation and commentary certainly rank as a serious literary achievement, whereas it might seem odd to apply to her exercises in Whimsey the criteria of literature, of great art. We might wish to protect her dramas from guilt by association and put them on the side of the translation as representing something more ambitious than her detective stories. Maybe. In what follows, I want to reflect a bit on our tendency to rank mystery fiction rather low on any literary scale, perhaps even to distinguish it radically from literature.

C. S. Lewis, in *Experiment in Criticism*, takes up this question and suggests that often the way we distinguish literature from what most people read most of the time is fairly snobbish. Literature is depicted as difficult or therapeutic. If it's enjoyable, it can't be serious, which is analogous to the Kantian notion that if something is the right thing to do it must be painful. To cut through all this, Lewis proposes as a preliminary working definition of literature the following: whatever we would read again. It is an inspired suggestion, I think, but it might seem to make short shrift of mysteries.

If mysteries are indeed whodunits, once we know how the story comes out, it would seem that our interest in them should be exhausted. Plot is certainly something fairly close to the skin of the mystery novel, and plot is the instrument whereby suspense and thus interest is created. There is a problem to be solved, and the story tells of the series of efforts, usually failed, to find the solution. Just when things look bleakest and the problem insoluble, our hero wins through and the story is over. Since a mystery turns on a murder, the problem is to discover the murderer. Once we know, we are unlikely to pick up the book again.

Plot being so prominent in mysteries—and in popular fiction generally—it is sometimes thought to be something vulgar and therefore absent from serious literature. E. M. Forster, a magnificent writer, tells us in *Aspects of the Novel* that he came to wish he could dispense with the need to tell a story in order to interest his reader. Story or plot, he felt, was a kind of pandering to a low-level reader. Well, Forster was a fastidious fellow, and his books are not exactly demotic in their appeal, but it is difficult to know just what he thought the removal of plot would leave him with.

It is more Aristotelian to maintain that plot is the soul of fiction and is indeed the logic of the events, that which confers on events their meaning. It is not, of course, the only element of fiction. But it is the vehicle on which are carried dialogue, description, theme, and all the rest. It may well be that, as Aristotle says, the writer is far more the maker of his plots than anything else, but I suspect that what captivates us in writers is their voice or vision, their peculiar way of seeing life. Books we read again and again—Lewis's definition of literature—have more than plot or suspense: indeed, since we already know how they turn out, the suspense initially felt is absent. At least once a year I read *Huckleberry Finn*. My memory isn't what it was, but I know how the story goes. Far from spoiling my pleasure, this enhances it. I can hardly wait to get to the extended section involving the Duke and the (late) Dauphin.

You will have long since seen what I am getting at. There are mysteries that we read again and again, and among them surely are those of Dorothy Sayers. (Needless to say there are straight or non-mystery novels that we do not care to read once, let alone again—rereadability is not decided by the genre.) The works of the great writers provide us with distinctive and illuminating meditations on the meaning of human life as exhibited in action. In drama. In doing. We are what we do, and the great writers in their very distinctive ways underscore the mysteriousness of human action.

The good that we would do, we do not, and the evil we would avoid, we do. Not only that, in doing what we intend, we bring about effects we do not intend, did not anticipate, happy and unhappy eventualities. Only self-made millionaires retain the notion that they are in complete control of their lives—and they are headed for a fall. Conrad's Lord Jim, Tolstoy's Prince André, Twain's Huck, Fitzgerald's Nick Carraway—on and on—put before us in various and concrete ways the human situation in a way we recognize as true.

Dorothy Sayers emphasized that Dante will be unintelligible to us if we think we are fated or if we think that the way we act does not matter. In Dante's world, our eternal fate is settled by what we do in the fleeing moments of time. After death, souls are what they have made themselves in life, and those in the Inferno are forever stuck with the selves they fashioned in life; in the Purgatorio, souls are better off, but they have before them the great task of cleansing themselves of the effects of their sins and imperfections. Heaven is their destination, so they retain the hope that has no place in hell. *Lasciate ogni speranza . . .*

I am putting this clumsily, but I think Flannery O'Connor was right to suggest that all literature points beyond the particulars it narrates to a meaning that transcends them. Reflecting as we are on the distinction between serious literature and such entertainments as mystery novels, we should acknowledge the sheepish feeling we often get when we realize how much of our lives is spent thinking of the imaginary deeds of nonexistent characters. Any concern with fiction can seem, to a certain kind of cold eye, trivial, culpable, childish. An academic colleague of mine once told me that he had heard I'd written a novel and went on to ask, concern in his eye, "It's not true, is it?" The implication being that, if it was true, I could hardly be a serious enough fellow to be a philosopher as well.

We all know the mood expressed in his question. The mood encompasses all fiction, not just mysteries. What's the answer? If our deeds were simply exhausted in their performance, gone without a trace, our interest in them would be fleeting at best. But it is the mark of the human agent that he is constantly stitching together the tenses of time, coming out of the past, projecting into the future, full of plans and aspirations, of proximate and long-term goals. We can do well or badly what we set out to do, but we can also set out to attain reprehensible goals. Our goals can be good or bad. Character is defined in terms of the goals sought as well as the success in attaining them. Indeed, there can be nobility in the failure to attain a lofty goal, just as success in the attainment of a depraved goal is itself a condemnation.

It is difficult not to make this sound moralizing, but it is not moralizing. Rather it is the explanation of why we ponder imaginary deeds. Such pondering is a kind of meditation on our common human situation. The tradition of our literature reposes on the conviction that the acts we perform are decisive for who we are. That haunting pair, Paolo and Francesca, encountered so early in the *Inferno*, arrest the postmodern—and perhaps even modern—reader. How can a stolen kiss (or more, as was likely the case, but even so) be commensurate with an eternal punishment? We may think infidelity so little a thing that we want to psychoanalyze Dante. All those years away from Gemma had to get to him. There must have been earthly Beatrices along the way. . . . Surely a little furtive and fugitive fondling can be eclipsed by the rest of one's life, made marginal, relatively unimportant?

It is that kind of attitude, Dorothy Sayers reminds us, that must be abandoned if we are to feel the force of Dante. I am suggesting that this is not at all peculiar to Dante. We don't have to inform the great Florentine about the divine mercy, the capacity to repent and alter our lives, indeed the ultimate good that can be brought out of our past misdeeds. He can teach us, and has, about all those things. But they too make sense only if action is serious.

You will smile and say that this sort of thing is absent from our fiction now. Perhaps. But it is difficult to think of it as being absent from mysteries and detective novels. For one human being to take the life of another human being is of unquestionable moment in the mystery. It is imperative that the one responsible be tracked down, apprehended, brought to justice. We are not permitted to wonder whether the pursuit of the wrongdoer is a worthwhile thing to do. Nor of course does this entail a simple black-and-white, good-or-bad division of characters. Often we are given a mordant view of the society within which the crime has been committed; the flaws in the best of the characters are revealed. But what is retained is the absolute distinction between good and evil.

If this sense had not weakened, Dorothy Sayers would not have had to instruct the readers of her translation of Dante. There is no longer a shared sense of what human action is, let alone what criteria there might be for assessing it as good or bad. It would be odd if our fiction did not reflect this. It would be odd if our fiction did not suffer from it. Here we find, I think, an explanation for the extraordinary preference for fiction that incorporates that view of the human person Dorothy Sayers recognized in Dante. When I started to publish, it would have been unheard of for a mystery or thriller to appear on the bestseller list, or at least it would have been so rare as to be noteworthy. Look at the lists today. Dorothy Sayers would recognize a kindred soul in Elmore Leonard. She would find Norman Mailer unintelligible.

Is this to be explained by that dogmatic air she detected in herself and, to a degree, deplored? In part, I suppose. The house of fiction is a commodious place, and those who live there bear only family resemblances to one another, sharing a nose, an ear, and eye, but seldom looking exactly alike. But common to the DNA of each inhabitant, if Dorothy Sayers is right, will be the recognition of the importance of action in determining who we are. It is to find out that, far more than to learn whodunit, that we go to fiction, including mystery fiction. Mysteries may be a poor relation in the house of fiction, but a lot that currently goes by the name of fiction will not even get through the door.

Even when they are reread, mysteries almost never do all the things that great novels do. Still, it is not necessary to falsely inflate their importance to see them as on the same spectrum as greater achievements. If the stock of mysteries has risen in our own day this is because of the parlous condition of fiction, its general lack of moral substance. We reread the Whimsey stories and to that degree they are literature, if Lewis is right; but it would be wrong to rank them higher than they deserve. What can be said of them is that they are continuous with the work and thought of Dorothy Sayers. This is why the reader who likes the tone and outlook of the mysteries will also enjoy her introductions and comments on Dante — and go on perhaps to read and savor *The Divine Comedy*. I suspect that she would regard that as the most gratifying result of all.

Dorothy L.'s Mickey Finn

H. R. F. KEATING

Perhaps the best thing Dorothy L. Sayers did for crime writing was not in giving the world its darling in the shape of Lord Peter Wimsey but in slipping us a great communal Mickey Finn. It came, long before other writers of Golden Age detective stories got around to it, in the form of simultaneous writing.

Simultaneous writing, common enough in the field of the mainstream novel, is the trick at one and the same time of telling your readers a simple ongoing story and of feeding them, all unknowing, with the material for inner meditation on one of the dilemmas that afflict us all as human beings. Let me illustrate its use first from a classic crime novel written long before the heyday of the mystery puzzle.

Wilkie Collins in *The Moonstone* told a story hard to put down, full of juicy characters, laced with humor, singing romantic love, properly cunning with clues ("Mr. Collins," said a snide reviewer at the time, "is nearly as clever as anyone who has ever fried a pancake in a hat") and, above all, one that holds us with the good old tug "Who Done It?"—in this case not who done a murder but the marvelously puzzling "Who stole the Moonstone?" But all the while Collins was doing something else as well. He was making us think about the dilemma we are all presented with by that terrible irrationality lurking just under the rational framework we all want to live within, the danger awaiting like the treacherous shivering sands that figure so prominently in the book. How can we come to terms with it?

It is those quicksands, glinting seductively, threatening death, that are the key to the way the Mickey Finn of a thought-provoking theme can be slipped into the mind of the mug. (That's us readers.) The powerful symbolism the sands hold does it. Collins, of course, larded his book with dozens of other resonating symbols, some large, some quite small. Chief among them, rightly, is the Moonstone itself, shimmering diamond worth thousands or, to quote, "mere carbon." As we take them all in, scarcely paying attention in the onward flow of the story, one by one they go to lie deep in our minds. And there they wait until, perhaps long after the book has been put back on the shelf, we wake in the night at first prey to fears, then somehow comforted.

Dorothy Sayers, once she had established herself as a producer of intriguing and flourishingly decorated detective stories (and made enough of the necessary pennies), adopted the same method. She had found she was a writer, a person gifted by dice-throwing chance with the ability to make maps of our chaotic old world and show us for a little the way things are. And as a writer she was impelled to give rein to the God-given gift.

She achieved this at its fullest, I believe, in her fifth book, *The Documents in the Case*, in 1930. But she had already explored the path two years earlier in the short story "Uncle Meleager's Will." A frivolous piece of work, you will say, with that gigantic crossword puzzle at its center, Dorothy Sayers indulging in academic play. How can this be anything to compare with what Wilkie Collins did in *The Moonstone*?

It is, of course, a frivolous piece of work. But it is also a meditation on the theme of frivolity, of how the human psyche is not complete without a counter-strain of fun to set against the seriousness with which it is necessary to approach the serious things life throws at us. I can go further and say the story is Dorothy Sayers's apology *pro vita sua*. With it she was saying, yes, I will write about theology, and, yes, I will one day translate that greatest and most serious of poems, Dante's *Divine Comedy*, but I have also written, and put into them the best of what I can do, entertaining detective stories.

So into this outwardly frivolous tale she put clues and hints and pointers to its theme, the importance of that streak of pure and simple fun. They are not deep-laid mines as Wilkie Collins's symbolic hints were. But they are rather little buried fireworks that as we step lightly on them, zipping through the story, alert us, later perhaps, to what it really has to say.

Look at the story in this light—a process almost as diverting, in fact, as reading it to see if one can beat wicked old Uncle Meleager (and brilliant Lord Peter) to the solution. First clue: the title. Why did Dorothy Sayers choose to give the maker of that will his curious forename? First because it sets the tone of the whole. It is a slightly ridiculous name for what, on the surface, is a slightly ridiculous piece of work. Then, too, it has a touch of the classical, and that again chimes in with the heart of the story, that monster crossword with its frankly learned clues. But Dorothy Sayers called her man Meleager for a hidden reason as well. Who was Meleager? Tell the truth, I had to look him up in the *Dictionary of Phrase and Fable* to find out. "Meleager. A hero of Greek legend, son of Oeneus of Calydon and Althaea, distinguished for throwing the javelin, for slaying the Calydonian Boar." Whoa, a boar. And who delighted in frivolous puns? DLS. So Meleager is the slayer of—what else?—a *bore*.

Right. Read the first few paragraphs. Bunter, the assiduously serious manservant, is doing a crossword! And Dorothy Sayers is saying it's all right for a hero, or one who is what the Hindi films call "a side-hero," to do something frivolous. If Bunter can, so we ought to be able to. And "Nonsense!" says Lord Peter. But that exclamation can cut two ways: it can condemn, but it can also simply describe. So we see nonsense as something, in some lights, as simply good.

Come next to the story's first long paragraph, a description of our great hero getting out of bed and moving toward the bathroom. "Every step he took . . . was a conscious act of enjoyment." Lesson to reader: enjoy the frivolities of this world, the delicate coils of steam rising from the awaiting, and frivolously late in the morning, bath. Another jab coming: Lord Peter sings a few bars of "Maman, dites-moi." In other words, he heralds the joys of innocent childhood, when all the world was fun.

On to Lord Peter, our spokesman, ordering his breakfast. Not bacon, "quite the wrong smell." But Bunter already has buttered eggs in mind, and his master at once agrees. "Excellent. Like primroses." So, although we have already been told it is June, we get the innocence of spring, gamboling lambs, a young man's fancy turning. One season of the four, then, tells us that to gambol is good.

Move on to Lord Peter's learning about the intricacies of Uncle Meleager's will, and to learning that Meleager's surname is Finch. A finch, a singing bird, and perhaps a subliminal reference to the Finches of the Grove, that on-the-edge-of-deplorable club young Pip joined in Dickens's *Great Expectations*. And what does Lord Peter exclaim when all is explained? "Uncle Meleager's a sport. I take to Uncle Meleager." A sport, a fun-lover. Indeed, a more direct, but worse, title for the whole story might be "The Importance of the Sportive."

We come next to the character of Hannah Marryat, the protagonist of the story, whose conversion from deadly seriousness is to be the crux of the whole. Lord Peter remembers her, "that intense young woman with the badly bobbed hair and the brogues." And his sister Mary chimes in frivolously with, "You could make it a condition of helping her that she should go and get properly shingled at Bresil's." Later Bunter is to find out from Uncle Meleager's remaining servants that "If a young lady came to see him, he'd like to see her hair shingled and the latest style in fashions." Fashion = frivolity.

Now Lord Peter dines at the serious, serious Soviet Club with Hannah and has a sudden intuition that if she were free from the importance of being earnest she would show great powers of enjoyment—flicked tribute to Oscar Wilde and his most frivolous, and enjoyable, play. A flick that surely, if only for a moment, brings to the reader all that Wilde at his most hedonistic stood for.

On to Uncle Meleager's letter, in which he reveals that a will written later than the one leaving everything to the Primrose League, "a body quite as fatuous as any other" (and one which Dorothy Sayers has already cued in with Lord Peter's primroses to Benjamin Disraeli, Conservative prime minister), can be superseded by the will he has ingeniously hidden. But it can be discovered only by some mysterious, frivolous means, since "I have always held that woman is a frivolous animal." And after that Soviet Club dinner what does Lord Peter invite Hannah to? To "the Pallambra." "I never go to music halls," says unfrivolous Hannah. But go she does. At the hero's bidding.

We come now, with Uncle Meleager's crossword clue-sheet unearthed but with no knowledge of where the diagram might be, to a highly significant moment: the baptism of Lord Peter. Not the religious ceremony that must once have been carried out, several bishops to hand, in the parish church at Denver, but another form of baptism, of the descent of enlightenment. Lord Peter falls into the little ornamental pool that is a feature of Uncle Meleager's odd house. He falls ingloriously, ridiculously, in. And emerges knowing the secret of the case. Strong enough moment of symbolism here, for all the comicality of the situation. "A splash and a flounder proclaimed that Lord Peter had walked, like Johnny Head-in-Air, over the edge of the impluvium." *Splash, flounder*: words that give the event an air of fun, reinforced by the Great Detective's being compared to the nursery-rhyme boy in *Struwwelpeter*:

> *Silly little Johnny, look*
> *You have lost your writing-book!*

But Lord Peter has not lost his writing-book. (If Uncle Meleager's clue-sheet had got soaked out of all recognition the whole story would have foundered.) Lord Peter has realized that the patterned tiles of the impluvium are Uncle's crossword, and the way is miraculously open for Hannah to become aware of—fun.

Two more of Dorothy Sayers's jabs at our minds and we have done. First the words with which Lord Peter comments on his discovery, "Oh frabjous day! Calloo! callay! I chortle." Lewis Carroll, of course, the master of nonsense, the master of nonsense with buried belowsense. Next, Hannah Marryat's last stand. They are solving one by one Uncle Meleager's decidedly difficult clues (I myself have cheated every time I have read the story and gone directly to the answers at the back) and Hannah says, "with a snort" when one of them has been solved, "That's just the kind of childish joke Uncle Meleager *would* make." Dorothy Sayers italicizes, in the interests of the story, that *would*, but had she wanted directly to draw attention to the meaning of the tale (as she would be wrong to do: these things have to work insidiously) the italics would have fallen on *childish*. That is, with the innocence and play of a child.

So much for that one short story. We come now to Dorothy Sayers's major attempt at simultaneous writing, *The Documents in the Case*. (She generously shared authorial credit with Robert Eustace, who gave scientific advice.) And here, too, the very title plays its part. The documents in the case: what that says, surely, is that here are things that can be believed, the documentary evidence. But we shall see as the book unfolds that they are the very opposite. Because the book is nothing less than a rumination on one of the philosophical dilemmas that have bemused mankind since the earliest days of the Greek or Indian civilizations, what the philosophers call the problem of reality.

How much that we see, hear, smell can we truly believe in? they ask. What else do we have when you come down to it but the evidence of our own sole, and fallible, senses? Boil away everything else and you eventually reach *Cogito ergo sum*, I only know that I exist because I am aware I am thinking. Or, to put it in the words of Dorothy Sayers's fellow theologian and fellow detective-story writer, Monsignor Ronald Knox,

> *There once was a man who said "God*
> *Must think it exceedingly odd*
> *If he finds that this tree*
> *Continues to be*
> *When there's no one about in the Quad."*

Dorothy Sayers abandoned Lord Peter for this book, and her doing so at the height of his popularity is a sign that she wished to clear the decks to undertake a difficult task. Because there can be no doubt about it, the task was difficult. She was undertaking to give her public what seemed to be, and was, a detective story, if one that asked not "Who done it?" but, more, "How on earth was it done?" How was George Harrison poisoned, if he was, when there was provenly no one present to cull the deadly fungi that poisoned him? And at the same time she wanted to plant in her readers' minds, so effectively that the thoughts stayed there, all that is implied by our human weakness of not knowing what is really true.

Her first expedient was to elect to tell her story in the form, chiefly, of letters, so that she could show us things from varying points of view. So the book opens, in a delightfully sprightly way, with a letter from one Agatha Milsom, spinster housekeeper at the Harrison London home, to her married sister. It begins with thanks for an inquiry after her health and a prompt comparison of her new doctor with her former one. Innocuous character demonstration? Not a bit of it. Dorothy Sayers uses it to play a little trick on us. By having Agatha state clearly that her new doctor is a man but refer to her old one simply as "Dr. Coombs," she leads us, by our stock response, to assume Dr. Coombs, too, is male. Only a few lines later to explode the idea with a sharp little "she." Things are not always what they seem, we learn.

In the course of this opening chatty letter other nudges are given to the underlying theme. There is a tiny reference to a psychoanalyst who, Miss Milsom says, seems to require all his patients to fall in love with him (we take this as gospel because it fits with our stock notion of the comic psychiatrist) and who "suffered so dreadfully from halitosis!" Point made: even godlike psychiatrists are all too human, can switch in a moment to being ordinary bad-breathed mortals.

The point is soon reinforced by a reference to George Harrison's wife, Margaret, always saying she is meant to have been born to wealth. (Point: we see ourselves as other than we are.) And the letter ends with a neat joke (a way of insinuating a serious point) by asking by implication: when is a pair of socks a cat? Answer: when the socks are knitted by Miss Milsom in a tortoiseshell pattern.

But before the book's end we discover that the Miss Milsom we have smiled at and have been led to sympathize with has all along been quietly going out of her mind. (Hence that tiny mention of the psychoanalyst.) Out of her mind: is she then herself, or who is she? Point made.

The second correspondent we read is one of two bachelors sharing a flat at the top of the Harrison house, John Munting, unpublished novelist (at the start of the book) and biographer. At once Dorothy Sayers gives herself a marvelous tool to lever her way down to the substance of her book. What is a biography but the asking "What truly was such-and-such a person?" and in John Munting's letters to his fiancée he can worry over the possibilities of achieving an answer to his (and Dorothy Sayers's) heart's content.

But Munting is used for more than this. Not only, of course, does he play a large part in the outward unraveling of the murder mystery but he also in later letters brings out the paradox that, while he is patently a solidly reliable chap and his flat-mate, Harwood Lathom, is very much the opposite, the household below them has, with complete verisimilitude, got the situation exactly reversed. (How mistaken can we get?)

This situation comes to a climax when, in the absence of George Harrison, Lathom, wearing Munting's dressing-gown on his way back from making love to Margaret Harrison, is mistaken in the dark by Miss Milsom for Munting, whom she then accuses hysterically of making advances to herself. Mistaken identity, characteristic device of farce and crime fiction, is here used for three purposes: to give us a welcome laugh, to provide a clue to the murderer, and, more important, to comment on the theme of the whole.

Time and again, in both major and minor ways, Dorothy Sayers prods us into thinking about the dilemma she wants to draw our attention to, whether as we read or even weeks and months afterward.

She has Lathom, who is an artist, paint Margaret Harrison and fall in love with her as he does so. And opportunity after opportunity arises to point out that a painter sees the true personality of a sitter, while in ordinary life a series of put-on personalities is offered to the world. (Question: which actually is the real person?)

Then George Harrison refuses to let the portrait be hung at the Royal Academy annual show. But Munting adroitly persuades him against his own judgment to change his mind. (Question: how much are our minds our own if an outsider can maneuver them?)

Harrison, a dry-as-dust fellow who is yet an imaginative cook (question: which is the real Harrison?) prepares a communal meal for the house and then, in a sulk, declares it is inedible so that nobody in the end eats it. (Question: was the meal really edible or inedible?)

Munting, accounting for sharing the flat with someone as different from himself as Lathom, recalls (useful plot point) that at school Lathom was noted for his ruthless acquisition of other boys' property. (Question: is there a real person inside us overlaid by the soft disguises of the years?)

Munting, thinking about Margaret Harrison, comes to see her as a prism, reflecting brilliant light from her lover's concentrated beam but seeming totally dull to those uninterested in her. (Question: which was she, truly?)

Lathom persuades Margaret to read D. H. Lawrence's *Women in Love* and she comments, with appropriate naïveté, "What funny people Lawrence's characters are! They don't seem to have ordinary lives. . . . I suppose the author means that the humdrum things don't really count." (Question: what does actually make up our lives?)

After Harrison is murdered Margaret, who thought she was going to have a baby by Lathom, finds she is not and reflects, "It's funny, I suppose if you and I really had a child, the law would have presumed it was his." (Question: brought up as a Harrison, would the child have become one? Next question: to what extent are we what we are purely legally?)

At the climax of the book Munting goes to dinner with the local

vicar, who happens (Dorothy Sayers had to stretch things somewhat for her purposes here) to have as his other guests old university friends, a top physicist, a biologist, and an up-and-coming
chemist. They discuss, of course, what makes the organic, the real,
different from the inorganic, the artificial, with a few Sayersy side-
swipes at the nature of belief. It is all, frankly, much too long-
winded (a Sayers weakness). Still, not only does it allow her to go
over the hidden ground of the book one last time—and in the light
of the then latest scientific thought—but in the middle of it all
Munting realizes that a remark by Waters, the chemist, might bear
directly on the murder.

They rush off to put the idea to experiment. The pace hots up.
The natural form of the poison that has killed Harrison is put in a
polariscope, and as happens with the natural product, white light
shines blazingly through. Powerful symbol. Then material from the
fungi dish Harrison prepared for himself is tested. And darkness,
black darkness. So the poison was not from fungi but was an artificial product and was added by the murderer to the broth Harrison
had prepared back at home. Murder plot and underlying theme
beautifully coming together at the finish. Dorothy Sayers triumphs.

The Comedy of
Dorothy L. Sayers

CATHERINE KENNEY

One of my favorite stories about Jane Austen describes an exchange between the verger at Winchester Cathedral and a visitor to that enormous edifice, where the novelist is buried. Bewildered by the number of queries he was receiving as to the exact location of Austen's grave, the curious verger is said to have asked of one literary pilgrim, "Can you tell me if there was anything special about that lady?" While it is true that half of the world will never understand the pleasures of the other, it is instructive for those of us who love a particular writer to be faced with such questions. Austen's value may appear self-evident to many readers, but many others cannot see what all the fuss is about. One need only attempt teaching her novels to be convinced of this truth. Similarly, some may wonder why Dorothy L. Sayers inspires such devotion among readers, and ask whether her work really deserves any special attention at all. Put boldly, is there good reason to celebrate her centenary with a collection such as this? Can we say that there was anything special about this lady?

The answer to this query would vary with every Sayers fan, and the range of articles included in this book suggests the myriad reasons for her enduring appeal. The fact that she can provoke other writers to think about so many different things, in so many different ways, is, in itself, indicative of her richness as an artist. Over the years, even those who have expressed antipathy toward Sayers have done so with gusto; none seems to find her boring. (See the critiques by Raymond Chandler and Julian Symons, for example.) Numerous writers have attested to her powerful influence upon them, including Carolyn Heilbrun (Amanda Cross), Simon Brett, H. R. F. Keating, Nina Auerbach, P. D. James, and Michael Gilbert. One cannot imagine the modern detective novel without her contributions, but her influence goes far beyond that genre into medieval and feminist studies as well as theology and social criticism. To call Sayers "a writer's writer" does not imply, as the term often does, that she is no longer read by general readers, or that she was preoccupied with form over substance. It is a simple acknowledgment of her strong effect on other writers and of the well-wrought nature of her created world.

The reasons for Sayers's appeal to other writers must be somewhat the same qualities that have provoked interest and esteem in the general readers she has always attracted in large numbers: her deft and memorable characterization; her ability to bring to life a new world, whole, incandescent, and throbbing with vitality; her insouciant gift for storytelling. All of this is embodied in a lucid, invigorating, and distinctive prose that is at once irresistible and inimitable, for Sayers is, above all else, a craftsman, an elegant and efficient wordsmith. In *Strong Poison*, Harriet Vane mocks her would-be suitor, Lord Peter Wimsey, by saying that if anyone ever marries him, it will be for the pleasure of hearing him "talk piffle," just as Sayers's readers are "married" to her work largely because they are attracted to her own wonderful and highly original voice. If her creations, including Wimsey, are absolutely unmistakable, so is she, and there is no better test of an authentic artist.

Perhaps the most distinctive characteristic of Sayers's voice, and the quality that evokes the most affection among readers, is its ebulliently comic tone. As Auden observed in his "Notes on the Comic," we may admire or like other people for many traits, but we tend to love those who make us laugh. We love being in their presence because they constantly remake the world anew by seeing it through the lens of comedy, and because laughter is, in itself, a healing art. We also tend to remember them well.

Dorothy L. Sayers seems to have been born with the true comic spirit, for it is in everything she ever wrote and is intrinsic to her way of seeing the world. Who but Dorothy Sayers can persistently get humor not only out of people and situations, but out of the intricacies of Christian theology, the translation of medieval poetry, or the economics of postindustrial Europe? Of how many scholarly editions could one possibly say what is true of her translation of Dante's *Divine Comedy*, that it is as entertaining as it is learned? This is not to suggest that she was anything but a serious scholar; in fact, it was the seriousness of her mind that enabled Sayers to see the profound comedy in the *Comedy*, and thereby make Dante more accessible to millions. The introductions and notes to her translation of *The Divine Comedy* are themselves a priceless repository of wit. Her description of Dante as a genius who was, like many other geniuses, "imperfectly house-trained," brings the long-dead poet to life more economically and suggestively than many more detailed biographical studies could do. Sayersian wit also enlivens the great play-cycle on the life of Jesus Christ, *The Man Born to Be King*. Consider, for example, her image of the biblical Rebecca, who is "in every sense a busybody—the indispensable woman with whom everybody would be happy to dispense." These pictures are surprising, especially given their manifestly serious contexts, and it is this very juxtaposition that yields the comedy. Indeed, a hallmark of Sayers's prose is the juxtaposition of what Thurber once called "the cosmic and mundane," which is at the heart of so much comedy.

Let's look at a representative Sayers passage to see how she exploits ironic juxtaposition and other classic comic techniques. It is the scene from *The Nine Tailors* in which the parish of Fenchurch St. Paul is meeting for services just after the discovery of a stranger's body in the churchyard:

> The service was devoid of incident, except that Mr. Venables again mislaid the banns, which had to be fetched from the vestry . . . and that, in his sermon, he made a solemn little allusion to the unfortunate

stranger whose funeral was to take place on the morrow, whereat Mr. Russell nodded, with an air of importance and approbation. The Rector's progress to the pulpit was marked by a loud and gritty crunching, which caused Mrs. Venables to mutter in an exasperated tone, "That's the coke again—Gotobed *will* be so careless with it."

Following the bland disclaimer that "the service was devoid of incident," the passage displays masterful comic timing as it piles irony upon irony: there is the juxtaposition of wedding banns (nearly lost, embarrassingly fetched before the entire village) and a funeral, which is described in classic comic understatement as being for the "unfortunate" stranger; the comic disparity between Venables's position and his problems with his memory and his staff; and finally, the clash between the sacred place and the mundane crunching of coke. In this brief passage, Dorothy Sayers, the vicar's daughter, has caught the essence of why we often suffer from suppressed laughter in church. She has also brought vividly to life not only Mr. and Mrs. Venables but the village undertaker, Mr. Russell, whose nod of "importance and approbation" is funny precisely because it is immediately recognizable to us from real life. These figures seem not to be created characters at all but human beings with lives of their own and an existence beyond the printed page. Only a writer with a deep sense of the eternal comedy of human life, and a genuine sympathy for her characters, could generate such a passage. And only one with considerable talent could make it seem so effortless.

Sometimes Venables himself employs comic timing, as when he chides Wimsey with the statement that "There's always something that lies behind a mystery. . . . A solution of some kind." This type of epigram also demonstrates the humor to be found in simply telling the bald, unadorned truth. We are so unused to honesty that it can startle us into laughter. Wimsey, the truth-seeker, excels at this form of humor, observing sardonically that "the great advantage about telling the truth is that nobody ever believes it." Another humorous aphorism from Wimsey is profound as well as comical: "There's nothing you can't prove if your outlook is only sufficiently limited." *Limited* is the last word one would expect at the end of this sentence, and the surprise of finding it there, as it overturns a proverbial truth, is humorous. On reflection, we can see that there is much truth to the statement, but only after we have been disarmed by laughter. We laugh at this kind of irony not because it represents an untruth, but because it expresses a reality that can be understood only by going against or beyond conventional thinking. Rather than dismissing such an idea with the notion that the speaker is "only joking," we must realize that a joke may be the most effective way of making a statement, albeit an indirect one. Since the two lines quoted above are from Sayers's penultimate and first novels respectively, one can safely say that this kind of verbal wit is characteristic not only of Wimsey, but of his creator.

Sayers took advantage of the raw power of truth-telling in her satiric essays on social criticism, which are as witty as her novels. Discussing "The Other Six Deadly Sins," she has this to say about modern morality:

> It was left for the present age to endow Covetousness with glamour on a big scale, and to give it a title which it could carry like a flag. It occurred to somebody to call it Enterprise. From the moment of that happy inspiration, Covetousness has . . . never looked back. . . . It looks so jolly and jovial, and has such a twinkle in its cunning eye, that nobody can believe that its heart is as cold and calculating as ever.

This is more lively and effective than much straightforward prose on the subject of greed, and it is certainly more arresting than the average theological text.

One of Sayers's essays on women, "The Human-Not-Quite Human," pushes us to see the inanity of gender stereotypes simply by treating the male animal as the female has always been treated. Imagining how an interviewer would describe a man in the new world order, she concocts this wonderfully satiric picture employing exaggeration, inversion, and comic timing to make its point: "There is nothing in the least feminine about the home surroundings of Mr. Focus, the famous children's photographer. His 'den' is panelled in teak and decorated with rude sculptures from Easter Island; over his austere iron bedstead hangs a fine reproduction of the 'Rape of the Sabines.' " As this passage shows, Dorothy Sayers understood well the potential for humor in any consideration of the sexes; indeed, her feminist writings are made much more palatable to most readers by the satiric tone in which they are cast. Humor permits a speaker to say more and go further than a straightforward statement can, and to Sayers's credit, she is usually good-humored as well as humorous on the subject of men and women. Her comic grasp of reality forces her to see both sexes as flawed and funny, rather than to engage in diatribes against men.

Sayers's own Wimsey, the purest expression of the wellspring of laughter that resided deep within her, is often the strongest voice for her revolutionary view of sexual politics, and it is a voice almost always tinged with comicality. The fact that Sayers casts a man as chief feminist both surprises and amuses us. Wimsey's admission to Harriet in *Gaudy Night* that "it is better fun to punt than to be punted, and that a desire to have all the fun is nine-tenths of the law of chivalry," not only helps disarm his lady, but also more effectively undermines the centuries-old male power structure than anger or direct assault could do. Like Dorothy Sayers herself, Peter Wimsey seems to laugh as other mortals breathe air. He goes so far as to define love as a comic art, avowing to Harriet that the "worst sin—perhaps the only sin—passion can commit, is to be joyless. It must lie down with laughter or make its bed in hell." How much contemporary fiction would benefit from a good dose of his philosophy! Wimsey represents one of the ways that comedy has of making the world anew, by simply seeing it without the blinders of received thinking and cliché, or by twisting conventional phrasing into puns, parodies, and other forms of wordplay.

Sayers uses puns to reveal character, to satirize literature and society, and to make serious comments indirectly, as well as to amuse. Many of her character names are wonderful puns: Wimsey and Vane themselves, of course, along with Gotobed, the church sexton; Miss Snoot, the schoolmistress; a secretary named Scoot; Miss Twitterton, who needs no explanation; Mr. Murbles, the lawyer whose name is a cross between murmur and babble; and a chimney sweep named Puffett. When Miss Climpson is accused of being a "Roaming Catholic" for her High Church ways, Lord Peter recognizes that the slip of the tongue suggests something about those Anglicans who looked longingly "toward Rome" in the early part of this century. Wimsey's mother, the Dowager Duchess of Denver, garbles one of Alexander Pope's most famous lines to the point that she ends up unexpectedly making another statement with which he would agree: "What oft was thought and frequently much better expressed, as Pope says—or was it somebody else? But the worse you express yourself these days the more profound people think you—though that's nothing new." The Dowager Duchess is hilariously confused about her sources, but she is devastatingly correct in her assessment of modern style. Then, in *The Documents in the Case*, we encounter the sublime Mrs. Cutts, whose malapropism, "excitements to murder," is only too appropriate for the tawdry love letters that lead to murder.

When Peter deliberately plays with the meanings of "head" and "heart" in the fourth chapter of *Gaudy Night*, Harriet tells him that he argues "like an Elizabethan wit—two meanings under one word." This is exactly his strategy, of course: to discuss not only acceptable subjects with her but an unacceptable one, indirectly through wordplay, as well. In so doing, his wit also addresses the central theme of the novel. Such is the elegant economy of comic repartee. Similarly, the bawdy puns offered in Bunter's toast to the newly wedded couple in *Busman's Honeymoon* reveal a humanity in the servant that we have not seen before and suggest a deep affinity between him and his master. The rollicking wordplay also helps set the tone for the Wimseys' wedding night, which is, by turns, funny, sexy, and emotionally mercurial. The fact that Wimsey's sister-in-law, Helen, Duchess of Denver, cannot keep up with such "rude rhymes" suggests the limitations of her character better than any description could. The fact that we learn this from the diary of Peter's mother makes it even funnier.

Risqué jokes are an expected part of the wedding ritual, but Sayers could use a pun like "The Importance of Being Vulgar" as the title for a serious literary essay. Invoking the ghost of Oscar Wilde, the title surprises us in its last word, which provides the hook to pull the reader into a treatise on language and literature. Sayers was a master of the provocative title and, while this essay does not argue exactly what we expect—that vulgarity in the common sense of profanity or pornography is important to art—it does make a strong point about the necessity for literature's appealing to the common emotions and desires of humanity. By implication, she is also talking about the importance of using the vulgate, or the language of everyday life. Sayers often uses such hyperbole to make a point, almost as if she feels it necessary for gaining our attention.

Just as verbal exaggeration can be very funny, comedy thrives on the exaggeration of predicaments. When Miss Climpson struggles with the moral question of whether to do something wrong in order to accomplish good, the narrator has a great deal of fun detailing every bit of the excruciating process of conscience. We understand the seriousness of Miss Climpson's predicament at the same time that we laugh at it; in fact, if she had not been in such a tight spot, the situation would not have been funny at all. Wimsey's long and painful pursuit of Harriet Vane is also funny, and even he has the insight to see himself as farcical in this role. Other notable examples of comic complication in the Sayers canon include the baroque forgetfulness of Venables and the Dowager Duchess; Bunter's overzealous care of Wimsey, his clothing, his reputation, and his port; the wild disarray of Miss Lydgate's monumental work of scholarship; and the ordeal of the chimney sweep in *Busman's Honeymoon*.

At the other end of the spectrum, comedy utilizes severe understatement as well, such as referring to a murder as "the unpleasantness at the Club," or the merry singing of Lord Peter, who has been made ecstatically happy by the discovery of a dead "body in a bath." These are examples of that peculiarly English pose of sangfroid in the face of death and disaster, like the Dowager Duchess's admission that "nobody can look her best in the dock at that dreary Old Bailey." A swing between the extremes of exaggeration and understatement is typical of the comic writer. As Thurber put it, the humorist "talks largely about small matters and smally about great affairs." The classic English detective story is in itself an example of this technique, stressing as it does the fine points of manners in a particular time and place while almost glancing over the fact that a violent crime is the reason for its plot.

Because of her close attention to the nuances of behavior and her scrutiny of the class system, it has become common for Sayers's critics to place her novels in the comedy of manners tradition. This is appropriate, and Sayers's own essays on detective fiction make it clear that she saw herself as working in that tradition. Like much of English literature, her novels are based largely in the comedy that arises out of class distinctions and domestic relations. The large Wimsey family itself, with all its history and alliances, provides an ample canvas on which to paint a microcosm of English society. As the books go through the years, we learn much about life as it was lived in England between the two great wars and see much to amuse us. We enjoy the laughter of derision at pretentious characters like Mrs. Gates, who makes a vulgar row over not being treated with respect, or Harwood Lathom, who sneers at suburbia while living out its worst clichés. Yet the Wimsey family, one of England's oldest, does not fare much better, with its beef-witted squire of an older brother, Gerald, his outrageous snob of a wife, and their irresponsible heir, Viscount St. George. Only a man like Peter Wimsey, the aristocratic renegade, could survive being born into such a family.

All comedy relies on the assumption that there are limits to acceptable human behavior, that there is such a thing as good and bad taste. But Sayers's novels go beyond questions of manners and mannerisms and into the realms of psychological realism and moral fable. They do this mainly through the developing persona of Lord Peter himself, who is portrayed at the beginning of the canon as a caricature of an English gentleman, but who grows into a well-defined human being with a complex inner life and all the ambiguities of a complete personality. What this shift means in terms of Sayers's comedy is that we progress from laughing *at* the external manifestation of a person and the situations in which he finds himself, to laughing *with* the character from inside his experience. Paradoxically, this internalizing of the comic vision also manages to shift the focus from the follies and whims of the individual character to the profoundly flawed nature of all human experience. The affectionate laughter evoked by such a comic apprehension of the world is perhaps most notable in the stories with Harriet Vane, who helped to humanize Peter by being a fully developed human being in her own right. For this reason, the only story they truly share, *Busman's Honeymoon*, is also Sayers's most mellow and subtle portrayal of the human comedy. And it is in the Vane-Wimsey quartet of novels that she actually uses the classic comic ending of wedding feast.

It is interesting that in her reviews of mysteries for the *Sunday Times*, published in the early 1930s, Sayers praised novels that had a comic touch but found most detective fiction of her day sorely lacking in humor. Her criticism also reveals that she understood the detective story as essentially comic in form, with its progress from disorder to order, or problem to solution, mimicking the classic happy ending of comedy. Her reviews and essays on detection are helpful in understanding her goals and standards as a novelist, and from her critical work we can deduce that she herself highly valued the comic sensibility.

When Sayers took on the task of interpreting *The Divine Comedy* in the early 1940s, she not surprisingly saw more humor in it than many other scholars have done. Like her fiction, the *Comedy* of Dante Alighieri is comic in this sense of humorousness, but more important, both writers share a profoundly comic vision of reality, a view that embraces the universe as it is and is essentially life-affirming. As a Christian, Sayers appreciated in Dante's poem the great comedy of redemption, the drama in which all comes round right at the end because of God's grace—a significant variation on the concept of Fortune that underlies classical comedy. Her own work is based in an understanding of the world as a flawed, funny, sometimes exasperating place that can yet be redeemed.

Sayers's world view, old-fashioned as it is, ironically helps explain the growing interest in her novels at this time and place in history. They are a tonic for us; with their sense of rightness, wholeness, and sanity, they recall some of the best qualities of eighteenth-century and nineteenth-century English fiction, and call us back to the idea that not only literature but life can be meaningful. Sayers's comic approach to the detective story puts her squarely in the tradition of the English novel, which has had a decidedly comic bent since Fielding defined *Joseph Andrews* as "a comic-epic poem in prose." One of the more surprising points in her consistently original look at Dante is her comparing him to Jane Austen, noting how these two very different comic artists were both blessed with a "central and abiding sanity." The comparison is very revealing, for it was this same central and abiding sanity that gave Sayers's own mind the stability and the rigor with which to create a comic universe. It has often been observed that comedy, like the detective story, appeals chiefly to the intellect. Thus it is not surprising that the keen, original, and generous mind of this supremely intellectual woman would see life as essentially comic.

Comedy has not flourished in all times and places, and although it is rarely appreciated as well as it should be, it is a difficult art. Like the love between two strong intelligences, the comic is always a matter of "very delicate balance." I would suggest that this is yet another reason for Sayers's popularity among writers, who of all people recognize the challenges of the comic form and appreciate good comedic writing when they see it. Yet Dorothy L. Sayers did not choose to approach the world comically, any more than she chose to be born at Oxford in the final decade of the last century; the comic voice and the comic vision were what she was. To appreciate her means to appreciate her comic art. In her discussion of Dante's *Paradise*, she writes that, when the poet finally reaches the place of supreme fulfillment, we realize along with him that "Humanity is not lost, [and] so . . . comedy is not lost." To be human means to be able, and to need, to laugh.

When Dorothy Sayers looked at life, she saw it from the comic distance, with that Olympian detachment characteristic of enduring comedy. Despite whatever pain and disappointment she had experienced, even perhaps because of them, she smiled back at the universe, just as she describes Dante smiling at the beatific vision that is the end of all journeys:

This is what he thought reality was like, when you got to the *eterna fontana* at the centre of it: this laughter, this inebriation, this riot of charity and hilarity. . . . Out of some inexhaustible spring in his fierce heart this great fountain of happiness comes bursting and bubbling.

And this is her gift to us. As sojourners in Sayers's world, we exult in such a "riot of charity and hilarity," and indeed sometimes get a glimpse of the inexhaustible spring that feeds it. Is it any wonder we love her so?

A Brief Biography of
Dorothy L. Sayers

A BRIEF SUMMARY OF HER life may help those who have not read any of the biographies. Born the only child of the Reverend Henry and Helen Mary Sayers in her beloved Oxford, she was four when her family moved to the Fens. While both parents early recognized her intelligence, it was her mother who not only was determined that Dorothy should have a university education but encouraged her to become a professional writer.

It was at Oxford University's Somerville College that she made the friends and established the pattern of her working life, for Sayers was not a solitary journal keeper but a letter writer who shared her work in progress with all interested friends, eagerly enlisting them in any current project. C. S. Lewis jokingly wrote her that if her letters were ever published she might find that her true fame rested upon them, not her published books. This has not happened yet because there are so many of them: over 30,000 pages in the Wade Center Collection alone. But in them you can hear the unmistakable Sayers voice, half poetic, half amused, describing the world about her with a discerning if tolerant eye, and the realistic details that created the ambience she called "particularity," the characteristic that has made her mysteries, firmly set in time and place, such excellent social history.

Dorothy later described herself as a child as a little prig, but she always showed her redeeming grace—a lively sense of humor. Despite an adult life with truly serious problems, including serving as the chief support for her illegitimate son as well as her "war-wounded" husband, Sayers maintained her energetic and enthusiastic manner, refusing to become a pessimist even when World War II, for which she and her generation felt responsible, broke out. Her innate sense of values, based upon the fundamental assumptions of Western civilization, were so much a part of her that, in talking about her as an artistic role model, each of the contributors to this book ends by discussing her philosophical point of view.

Out of college Sayers taught, tried publishing, then took a copywriting job in London about the time her first mystery, *Whose Body?*, appeared in print. Lord Peter Wimsey, created to be her breadwinner, did so nobly. But as she became better known and got her toe inside the stage door, where everyone was a comrade in arms working toward a common goal, her desire to keep churning out a mystery or two each year flagged. Her interest in the Wimseys themselves never ended, but she kept them for her spare time and close friends, as she, thanks to World War II, became more and more involved in war work. She began to write plays on more obviously religious themes, particularly her magnificent cycle on the life of Christ, which made him real to the mid-twentieth century. This was followed finally by her great gift to the postwar world, her lively translation of Dante. His work (and personality) fit her own so very well that her friend Barbara Reynolds argues convincingly that it was Dante the writer, not Lord Peter, the fictional lord, who was her ideal man.

When Sayers died suddenly of a stroke on December 17, 1957, she left *Paradise* unfinished, to be completed by Barbara Reynolds, the latest in the long list of Sayers's devoted friends.

Notes on the Contributors

CATHERINE AIRD is a past chairman of the British Crime Writers Association, a member of the Dorothy L. Sayers Society, and the author of a series of detective stories starring Inspector C. D. (Seedy) Sloan of the Calleshire Constabulary. She is working on a biography of Josephine Tey and is convinced that Chaucer wrote a detective story. According to her, any resemblance between her fictional "Calleshire" and her native Kent is purely coincidental, despite the fact that her house in Sturry has a "lethal" newel-post like the murder weapon in *The Religious Body*.

ALZINA STONE DALE read her first Dorothy L. Sayers mystery in college and never looked back. She has published a biography of Sayers called *Maker and Craftsman*, to be reissued for the Sayers Centennial; edited *Love All*, a collection of Sayers's comedies; and spoken on Sayers from London to Seattle. Her hobby is writing the *Mystery Readers Walking Guides*, which allow the avid fan to follow his favorite sleuth's footsteps through London, New York, and England.

AARON ELKINS is a former anthropology professor best known for his witty and engaging Gideon Oliver mysteries, which feature "the skeleton detective." A TV series was adapted from the Oliver series, and his *Old Bones* won an Edgar from the Mystery Writers of America. Guest of Honor at the Malice Domestic IV mystery convention, he also has a series on the art world, which stars Chris Norgren, a curator of the Seattle Art Museum, and has written a golfing mystery with his wife, Charlotte.

MICHAEL GILBERT is a former Lincoln's Inn solicitor. Not only was he initiated into the Detection Club by Dorothy L. Sayers herself, and with Michael Innes is one of its oldest members, but he was also a founder of the British Crime Writers Association. One of his best-known mysteries is

Smallbones Deceased, in which a client is murdered in a law office and filed for future reference. In addition to being named a Grand Master by Mystery Writers of America for his lifetime achievement in writing about crime, he was awarded the C.B.E. in honor of both his legal and writing careers. Many of his mysteries were written when he commuted daily from Kent to London, but he says that he has retired from the law, though not from writing.

CAROLYN G. HART is a past president of Sisters in Crime. Her detective, Annie Laurance, not only runs the perfect mystery bookstore, called Death on Demand, but teaches classes in the genre. Annie also directs mystery plays, creates mystery weekends, and with her charming and wealthy husband, Max Darling, put on *The Christie Caper*, a mystery convention dedicated to Sayers's contemporary, Agatha Christie, which explored the nature of biography. Hart's mysteries have won Anthony, Macavity, and Agatha awards.

CAROLYN G. HEILBRUN is the former Avalon Foundation Professor in the Humanities at New York's Columbia University. A past president of the Modern Language Association and an English professor for thirty-two years, she recently resigned over the continued refusal of the "old boy network" to allow equal tenure opportunities for women. This Sayersian-style battle will come as no surprise to the many fans of her highly literate mysteries starring the feminist Professor Kate Fansler, which Heilbrun writes as "Amanda Cross." Nor will it startle those of us who heard her spirited defense of Sayers as a feminist role model in *"Gaudy Night* and Its American Women Readers"* read before the Sayers Society at Somerville College, Oxford, in August 1985.

H. R. F. KEATING is not only the current president of the Detection Club and a past chairman of the Crime Writers Association and the Society of Authors, but is also a well-known mystery reviewer and critic. He is the creator of a series starring the Bombay CID's Inspector Ghote and has won both a Golden Dagger and an Edgar. He is also trying to collect and record the history of the Detection Club, to which Sayers and her friend Helen Simpson devoted so much time and energy.

CATHERINE KENNEY is the author of *The Remarkable Case of Dorothy L. Sayers*, a study of Sayers as a woman of letters that was nominated for an Edgar. She has also written a book on James Thurber, *Thurber's Anatomy of Confusion*, as well as numerous stories and articles. A member of The

Jane Austen Society, she teaches literature at Loyola University of Chicago.

WILLIAM F. LOVE has been a monk, a Roman Catholic priest, a banker, and now a writer who is also interested in theater and has his own show on cable TV. All his pasts were grist for his mill when he created his Nero Wolfe–like series about New York's handicapped Bishop Francis X. Regan and his live-in "Archie," ex-cop Davy Goldman. *The Chartreuse Clue* was nominated for an Agatha. He is a member of MWA and Sisters in Crime.

SHARYN MCCRUMB is a southern novelist whose mysteries wickedly and wittily explore the politics of folklore and culture. A member of the Appalachian Studies faculty at Virginia Tech, she won an Edgar for *Bimbos of the Death Sun* and an Agatha for "A Wee Doch & Doris."

RALPH MCINERNY is a professor of philosophy at the University of Notre Dame, South Bend, Indiana, where he is also known as an authority on G. K. Chesterton. He is not only the creator of the Father Dowling mysteries seen on TV and the Andrew Broome series, but as "Monica Quill," he writes about Sayers look-alike Mother Superior "Emmtee" or Sister Mary Theresa Dempsey, whose order (with only three other nuns left) lives in a Frank Lloyd Wright house in Chicago. As "Edward Mackin" he recently published an ironic academic mystery, *The Nominative Case.*

ANNE PERRY is a Londoner who now lives on the northeastern coast of Scotland in an ancient house, which she has renovated. She considers G. K. Chesterton's whimsical *The Man Who Was Thursday* her favorite book, showing she shares the tastes of Dorothy L. Sayers. She is well known for her Victorian mystery series starring Scotland Yard Inspector Thomas Pitt and his wife, Charlotte, which, like many of Chesterton's Father Brown mysteries, exposes the layers of social hypocrisy. She was nominated for an Agatha for her tour de force *The Face of a Stranger*, which featured a London police detective called William Monk.

B. J. RAHN is a member of the English department of Hunter College of the City University of New York. She has been teaching, researching, and writing about crime fiction for the past decade. She is cofounder of *Murder Is Academic*, a newsletter for people teaching crime fiction at the college level. She is a member of the Mystery Writers of America, the Sherlock Holmes Society of London, and the Crime Writers Association of the United Kingdom.

IAN STUART, who also writes under the name "Malcolm Gray," has retired from the business world to pick up where he left off as a schoolboy devoted to the mystery story. As a member of the CWA he welcomed most kindly some strange Americans to a meeting in Shoe Lane, London, despite a sinister reference in one mystery to a determined Chicagoan who had triumphantly "invaded" the obscure village her ancestors came from. But his tolerance for American mystery writers who pretend to be authorities on things British is very low, and he enjoys listing the errors in their best-selling texts in long letters to his American friends.

Selected Bibliography

THE TWO BIBLIOGRAPHIES LISTED first contain the sources of all the published writings of Dorothy L. Sayers. As yet, there is no complete listing of her unpublished works and letters. The best place to find copies of her writing as well as most of her unpublished work is at the Wade Center, Wheaton College, Wheaton, Illinois 60187. This is a noncirculating collection open to all fans and researchers free of charge. The other main source of Sayersiana is the collection of the Dorothy L. Sayers Society. For more information about their holdings, write to Christopher Dean, Sayers Society, Rose Cottage, Malthouse Lane, Hurstpierpoint, West Sussex, BN6 9JY, England.

Gilbert, Colleen B. A. *Bibliography of the Works of Dorothy L. Sayers.* New York: MacMillan, 1978.

Harmon, Robert B., and Margaret A. Burger. *An Annotated Guide to the Works of Dorothy L. Sayers.* New York: Garland Publishing, 1977.

WORKS OF DOROTHY L. SAYERS, IN
CHRONOLOGICAL ORDER
Op I. Oxford, 1916.
Catholic Tales and Christian Songs. Oxford, 1918.
Whose Body? New York, 1923.
Clouds of Witness. London, 1926.

Unnatural Death. London, 1927.

The Unpleasantness at the Bellona Club. London, 1928.

Introduction to *Great Short Stories of Detection, Mystery and Horror.* (Omnibus of Crime). London, 1928.

Lord Peter Views the Body. London, 1928.

Tristan in Brittany. London, 1929.

The Documents in the Case. London, 1930.

Strong Poison. London, 1930.

"Behind the Screen," BBC radio serial by the Detection Club, 1930.

"The Scoop," BBC radio serial by the Detection Club, 1931.

The Five Red Herrings. London, 1931.

Introduction to *Great Short Stories of Detection, Mystery and Horror— Second Series.* London, 1931.

The Floating Admiral. Detection Club, London, 1932.

Have His Carcase. London, 1932.

Murder Must Advertise. London, 1933.

Hangman's Holiday. London, 1933.

The Nine Tailors. London, 1934.

Introduction to *Great Short Stories of Detection, Mystery and Horror— Third Series.* London, 1935.

Gaudy Night. London, 1935.

Busman's Honeymoon, with Muriel St. Clare Byrne. London, 1937.

Busman's Honeymoon. London, 1937.

The Zeal of Thy House. London, 1937.

The Devil to Pay. London, 1939.

In the Teeth of the Evidence. London. 1939.

He That Should Come. London, 1939.

"Wimsey Papers" in *The Spectator.* London, 1939–40.

Begin Here. London, 1940.

Love All, performed London, 1940. Kent, Ohio, 1984.

The Mind of the Maker. London, 1941.

The Man Born to Be King, performed 1941–42. London, 1943.

Even the Parrot. London, 1944.

The Just Vengeance. London, 1946.

Unpopular Opinions. London, 1946.

Creed or Chaos. London, 1949.

The Comedy of Dante Alighieri: Hell. London, 1949.

The Emperor Constantine. London, 1951.

Introductory Papers on Dante. London, 1955.

The Comedy of Dante Alighieri: Purgatory. London, 1955.

Further Papers on Dante. London, 1957.

The Song of Roland. London, 1957.

The Comedy of Dante Alighieri: Paradise. Completed by Barbara Reynolds. Published posthumously, London and Baltimore, 1962.

The Poetry of Search and the Poetry of Statement. Published posthumously, London, 1963.

Lord Peter. New York, 1972.

Wilkie Collins. Incomplete biographical study. Edited by E. R. Gregory, Toledo, Ohio, 1977.

The Whimsical Christian. Edited by William Griffin. New York, 1978.

Love All. Edited by Alzina Stone Dale. Kent, Ohio, 1984.

SELECTED SECONDARY SOURCES

Brabazon, James. *Dorothy L. Sayers: A Biography.* New York: Charles Scribner's Sons, 1981.

Brittain, Vera. *Testament of Experience.* 1957. Reprint, New York: Wideview Books, 1981.

———. *Testament of Friendship.* 1940. Reprint, New York: Seaview Books, 1981.

———. *Testament of Youth.* 1933. Reprint, New York: Wideview Books, 1980.

———. *Women at Oxford: A Fragment of History.* New York: Macmillan, 1960.

Brunsdale, Mitzi. *Dorothy L. Sayers, Solving the Mystery of Wickedness.* New York: Berg, 1990.

Byrne, Muriel St. Clare. *Garden or Common Child.* London: Faber & Faber, 1942.

———, ed. *The Lisle Letters.* Chicago: University of Chicago Press, 1981.

Byrne, Muriel St. Clare, and Catherine Hope Mansfield. *Somerville College*. Oxford: Oxford University Press, 1921.

Carpenter, Humphrey. *The Inklings, C. S. Lewis, J. R. R. Tolkien, Charles Williams, and Their Friends*. London: George Allen and Unwin, 1978.

Dale, Alzina Stone. *Maker and Craftsman, The Story of Dorothy L. Sayers*. Grand Rapids, Mich.: Wm. B. Eerdmans Publishing, 1978. Revised edition, Wheaton, Ill.: Harold Shaw Publishers, 1992.

———. *The Outline of Sanity, A Life of G. K. Chesterton*. Grand Rapids, Mich.: Wm. B. Eerdmans Publishing, 1982.

———. *T. S. Eliot, the Philosophy Poet*. Wheaton, Ill.: Harold Shaw Publishers, 1988.

Dean, Christopher, ed. *Encounters with Lord Peter*. Published by the Dorothy L. Sayers Society, Hurstpierpoint, West Sussex, 1991.

Frankenburg, Charis U. *Not Old, Madam, Vintage*. Lavenham, Suffolk: Galaxy Press, 1975.

Gaillard, Dawson. *Dorothy L. Sayers*. New York: Unger, 1981.

Hall, Trevor. *Dorothy L. Sayers: Nine Literary Studies*. London: Duckworth, 1980.

Hannay, Margaret, ed. *As Her Whimsey Took Her*. Kent, Ohio: Kent State University Press, 1979.

Haycroft, Howard, ed. *The Art of the Mystery Story*. New York: Carroll & Graf Publishers Inc., 1946, 1983.

Heilbrun, Carolyn G. *Writing a Woman's Life*. New York: W. W. Norton, 1988.

Hitchman, Janet. *Such a Strange Lady: An Introduction to Dorothy L. Sayers*. London: New English Library, 1975.

Hone, Ralph. *Dorothy L. Sayers, A Literary Biography*. Kent, Ohio: Kent State University Press, 1979.

Jakubowski, Maxim, ed. *100 Great Detectives or the Detective Directory*. New York: Carroll & Graf Publishers, 1991.

Kenney, Catherine. *The Remarkable Case of Dorothy L. Sayers*. Kent, Ohio: Kent State University Press, 1990.

Leonardi, Susan J. *Dangerous by Degrees. Women at Oxford and the*

Somerville College Novelists. New Brunswick, N.J.: Rutgers University Press, 1989.

Lewis, C. S. "Panegyric for Dorothy L. Sayers," in *Of Other Worlds.* London: Collins, 1982.

Reynolds, Barbara. *The Passionate Intellect.* Kent, Ohio: Kent State University Press, 1989.

Scott-Giles, C. W. *The Wimsey Family.* London: Victor Gollancz, 1977.

Sprague, Rosamund. *A Matter of Eternity.* Grand Rapids, Mich.: Wm. B. Eerdmans Publishing, 1973.

Symons, Julian. *Mortal Consequences.* London: Faber & Faber, 1972.

Tischler, Nancy. *Dorothy L. Sayers, A Pilgrim Soul.* Atlanta, Ga.: John Knox Press, 1980.

Woolf, Virginia. *A Room of One's Own.* New York: Harcourt, Brace, 1929.

Index